The Problem of Democracy

THE PROBLEM OF
DEMOCRACY

Alain de Benoist

ARKTOS

MMXI

First English edition published in 2011 by Arktos Media Ltd., originally published as *Démocratie: le problème* (Paris: Le Labyrinthe, 1985).

Printed in the United Kingdom

ISBN 978-1-907166-16-7

BIC classification: Social & political philosophy (HPS)
Political structures: democracy (JPHV)

Translator: Sergio Knipe
Editor: John B. Morgan
Cover Design: Andreas Nilsson
Layout: Daniel Friberg
Proofreader: Matthew Peters

ARKTOS MEDIA LTD

www.arktos.com

TABLE OF CONTENTS

A NOTE FROM THE EDITOR. 7

PREFACE BY TOMISLAV SUNIC. 9

I. THE ANCIENTS AND THE MODERNS. 13

II. A DEFENCE OF DEMOCRACY. 30

III. POPULAR SOVEREIGNTY AND PLURALISM 54

IV. THE CRISIS OF DEMOCRACY. 72

V. TOWARDS ORGANIC DEMOCRACY 93

POSTFACE: TEN THESES ON DEMOCRACY 100

A NOTE FROM THE EDITOR

Alain de Benoist's text already contained a substantial number of footnotes, all of which have been retained for the present edition. To these I have added additional footnotes where I felt they would be helpful, either to explicate references or to allow the reader to more deeply explore de Benoist's sources. Notes added by myself are so indicated, while notes with no indicator are part of the original text. Also, wherever texts have been referenced, they have been replaced by references to the English-language originals or translations, when they are available. Works that have not been translated are retained in their original language.

When reading the text, please keep in mind that de Benoist originally wrote and published this book in 1985.[1] Although the developments during the intervening years in no way detract from the value of his observations, he does make occasional reference to contemporary circumstances which no longer exist, in particular the Soviet domination of eastern Europe.

Finally, both the translator and the editor wish to acknowledge the assistance they received by consulting Dr. Tomislav Sunic's previous translation of the first chapter of this book, which was published in the Summer 2003 issue of *The Occidental Quarterly*. Although this book, including the first chapter, is an entirely original translation, Dr. Sunic's text was extremely valuable in clarifying some passages.

– JOHN B. MORGAN

---

1   *Démocratie: le problème* (Paris: Le Labyrinthe, 1985).

PREFACE

Those who love to regurgitate the word 'democracy' are usually those who know little about its meaning in the first place. One could draw a parallel with a criminal on trial who never calls himself a crook. It is only his accusers who call him a crook. De Benoist rightly states that every single political actor today, regardless of which corner of the Earth in which he may dwell, likes to decorate himself with the noun 'democracy'. Every tiny criticism of that word, each skeptic who doubts its current methods of employment, is immediately denounced as undemocratic. Even discussing the notion of our modern liberal democracy means to step onto the minefield of a new religion, whereas making any critical comment about modern liberal democrats is tantamount to intellectual suicide.

The noun 'democracy' works miracles, to the point that its four syllables, 'de–mo–cra–cy', when loudly uttered in public, easily disarm any of its adversaries and dismiss all of its critics. This word, especially when inscribed on the banner of the modern liberal system, can also become the ideal cover for the most despicable political crimes. In recent history it came in handy as an alibi for carrying out serial killings against custom-designed non-democratic political actors. Or, for that matter, its loftier expression, such as 'fighting for democracy', can serve beautifully as a safe venue for firebombing entire 'non-democratic' nations into submission. The surreal beauty that this generic noun implies, based on the specific time and place of its user, can mean everything and nothing at the same time. Today, this noun and its democratic qualifiers have become part and parcel of every politician's lexical arsenal. God forbid if a politician in the West dares to voice critical views of its quasi-religious significance! Not long ago, the Christian masses in Europe were obliged to chant 'cantate domino' in order to reassure themselves, amidst their suspicious co-religionists, of their eternal devotion to the singular Lord in Heaven, and thus avoided the risk of being chastised as heretics, or being burned at the stake as devils incarnate. Back then, nobody wanted to be ratted out for seeing the shortcomings of *the* dominant belief, or kicked out of his community for being out of the monotheist loop! Hallelujah!

Similar fancy buzzwords, such as 'Son of Yahweh', and a plethora of other Levantine sermons from Sinai, are still heard amidst the enraptured congregations of the Bible Belt. These words are still in use as the pious trademarks of the chosen people. Short of that, for an agnostic or a more urbane layman, the divine word 'democracy' can work miracles if he is desperately scrambling for an effective way to complete his dangling and embarrassing sentence. An American serial killer often discovers an alibi for his misdeeds by invoking loudly in court, 'God made me do it!' We should not blame him too harshly. During the Second World War the self-proclaimed democratic world-improvers, both from the east and from the west, used the normative principles of democratic limitations to justify large-scale killings and expulsions – and the exclusion of their non-democratic foes. Tomorrow, should the Third World War break out, it will likely be rationalised by the adherents of democracy, who will invoke the already well-tested phrase, 'Let's make the world safe for democracy!'

Yes, that was the word in the beginning. And then came the ugly deed. It is therefore a merit of the philosopher Alain de Benoist that before tackling the concept of the political within the democratic system, he first deals with the etymology of the word and its semantic deviations and aberrations in different historical epochs. After following his narrative, which he skillfully outlines in this little book, one can only come to the conclusion that the current overuse of the word 'democracy' often results in inter- and infra-political mayhem which will likely bring about political catastrophes in the near future.

All those who are familiar with Alain de Benoist's books know very well that all of them are instructive. They represent a treasure trove of various ideas, ranging from literature, art, and history to political science, and they all attest to a man of classical erudition. This little book on democracy is especially important, because it directly examines a mystical term of our times and which recurs in our daily communication. The notion of modern democracy, which Alain de Benoist dissects in detail, is not just a label for a form of (anti-)government; it is first and foremost a label for the all-encompassing imagery which is being projected for the benefit of the public; a pervasive system of symbolism which even an uneducated man from the street must confront on a daily basis.

There are several reasons why this book is obligatory reading for any student of democracy – let alone for undergraduate students in the humanities. First there is the language of the book. Alain de Benoist's style is always limpid with a simple, didactic message. His style is not an arcane one designed for a chosen few. Even when reading him in an English translation, it does not pose a massive headache for a novice. A reader does not need to be versed in high-tech political jargon in order to understand his main thesis – as is often the case with many 'experts' hiding behind flowery and vague sentences, often in an attempt to conceal their substantial ignorance.

De Benoist puts his description of democracy into a larger perspective and he observes its genealogy from a linguistic, historical and sociological perspective. The value of this book lies in the fact that it demystifies or 'deconstructs' the contemporary verbiage surrounding the notion of democracy. It helps us to realise how our own conceptualisation of democracy has been hijacked over a long period of time by a destructive, linear way of thinking. The underlying assumption, which de Benoist denounces (albeit the assumption that is still held by many academics), is that our liberal democracy, often tagged with the lexical barbarism of 'free market democracy', represents the best of all possible worlds and that everything preceding its appearance must be discarded as obsolete or 'undemocratic'. De Benoist, in his impressive bibliography, offers the reader substantial proof that this so-called democracy of ours may actually be the worst of all possible worlds.

This book is important insofar as the author, when he wrote it in 1985, had a premonition of how liberal 'market democracy' would later become the very opposite of what it was supposed to be. Democracy means participation in political affairs. However, in view of the mediocre voter turn-outs which occur all over Europe and the United States, one must raise serious questions about the legitimacy of what is called today 'modern liberal democracy'. Frankly, both in the east and the west as well as the United States, the vast majority of voters have a rather negative opinion of their democratically elected officials. Is this not a good enough reason to critically examine the notion of modern democracy?

De Benoist rightly states that democratic principles have been major ingredients in Europe – from Antiquity all the way to modern times – regardless of the various, and often 'undemocratic' signifiers our ancestors ascribed to their regimes. In the forums of ancient Greece or in Thingsvellir in ancient Iceland, our ancestors knew how to use the democratic method for electing their leaders and deciding their public affairs. Conversely (and this is something the reader must particularly bear in mind when reading this book), the most visible and the most vocal democrats in our age have often been individuals and systems of the most despotic and despicable character. Witness, for example, the ex-democratic Soviet Union with its purportedly democratic Constitution of 1936!

At the very least, this book is a useful work of scholarship which urgently needs to be perused by the postmodern ruling class and by all students wishing to decipher the mechanisms of the dying liberal system. The additional asset of this book is that it is not a propaganda piece. It is not a pamphlet; nor does it endorse a specific political or ideological agenda. However, this precious book surely does offer some quick clues as to how we need to proceed while we are submerged in the bombastic rhetoric about democracy in our times.

Recently, Alain de Benoist made a short summary of our modern liberal democracy: 'We live in an oligarchic society where everybody pretends to be a democrat – but where there is no democracy.'

Tomislav Sunic
Zagreb, Croatia
December 28, 2010

I

THE ANCIENTS AND THE MODERNS

'The defenders of every kind of regime claim that it is a democracy', George Orwell observed.[1] This is nothing new. Already in 1849, Guizot had written, 'Such is the power of the word Democracy, that no party or government dares to raise its head, or believes its own existence possible, if it does not bear that word inscribed on its banner'.[2] This is truer today than ever before. Not everyone today is democratic, but everyone purports to be: there is not a single dictatorship that does not claim to possess a democratic spirit. The Communist countries of eastern Europe present themselves not merely as democracies—something attested by their very constitutions[3]—but as the only *real* democracies, as opposed to the 'formal' democracies they identify with the liberal democracies of the West.

This almost unanimous consent given to democracy as a word—if not always on the thing itself—gives the notion a *moral* and quasi-religious meaning, which discourages discussion right from the start. Many authors have stressed this fact. In 1939, T. S. Eliot stated, 'When a term has become so universally sanctified as "democracy" now is, I begin to wonder whether it means anything, in meaning too many

---

1   George Orwell, *A Collection of Essays* (Garden City, New York: Doubleday, 1954), p. 162.

2   François Guizot, *Democracy in France* (London: John Murray, 1849), p. 3.

3   Georges Burdeau notes that 'judging from appearances, the political institutions of the USSR are very similar to those of the United States in terms of federal organisation, and to those of the United Kingdom in terms of system of government', in *La démocratie* (Paris: Éditions du Seuil, 1966), p. 141.

things.'[4] Even more sharply, in 1945 Bertrand de Jouvenel affirmed, 'All discussions of democracy, all arguments whether for or against it, are stricken with intellectual futility, because the thing itself is indefinite.'[5] Giovanni Sartori added in 1957, 'In a somewhat paradoxical vein, democracy could be defined as a high-flown name for something which does not exist.'[6] Finally, Julien Freund noted (not without a touch of humour), 'To claim that one is a democrat no longer means a thing, as it is possible to be democratic in contradictory ways, whether in the manner of the Americans or British or in that of the Communists of eastern Europe, Congo and Cuba. Given these circumstances, it is quite natural that I should refuse to be democratic, as my neighbour can invoke the same word, even if he supports a dictatorship.'[7]

Clearly, the universal nature of the term does not particularly help to clarify its meaning. Undoubtedly, we need to go one step further.

The first idea we must do away with is the notion of certain people who claim that democracy is a specifically modern product, corresponding to the most 'developed' stage in the history of political regimes.[8] Any such idea is unsubstantiated. Democracy is neither more 'modern' nor more 'developed' than any other regime. Democratic regimes or tendencies can be found throughout history. Once more, the linear view of history here proves particularly misleading. In relation to political regimes, the very idea of progress is meaningless.

For the same reason, we cannot accept the idea of the 'naturalness' of democracy, whereby certain liberals would have us believe that democracy 'spontaneously' arises in the political sphere, just as the market 'spontaneously' arises within the logic of trade. Thus, according to Jean Baechler, 'If we acknowledge that humans, as a species of animal [sic], spontaneously aspire to a democratic regime that promises safety, prosperity and liberty, we are forced to conclude that as soon as the right conditions have been met, the democratic experience

---

4   T. S. Eliot, *Christianity and Culture* (New York: Harcourt, Brace & World, 1949), p. 11. (Ed.)

5   Bertrand de Jouvenel, *On Power* (Boston: Beacon Press, 1962), p. 276.

6   Giovanni Sartori, *Democratic Theory* (Detroit: Wayne State University Press, 1962), p. 3.

7   'Les démocrates ombrageux', in *Contrepoint*, December 1976, p. 111.

8   Other authors have held exactly the opposite opinion. According to Schleiermacher, democracy is a 'primitive' political form, monarchy being the only one capable of meeting the needs of the modern state.

will spontaneously emerge, without the need for any appeal to ideas.'[9] What, then, are these 'conditions' that produce democracy, just as fire produces heat? Clearly, nowhere is this specified.

In contrast to the Orient, absolute despotism has always been exceedingly rare in Europe. Whether in Rome, in the *Iliad*, in Vedic India or among the Hittites, already at a very early date we find the existence of popular assemblies for both military and civil organisation. Moreover, in Indo-European society the King was generally elected: all ancient monarchies were initially elective. Tacitus[10] relates how among the Germanic tribes, 'They choose their kings for their noble birth, their commanders for their valour'[11] (*reges ex nobilitate, duces ex virtute summunt*). Even in France, the crown long remained both elective and hereditary. It was only with Pippin the Short[12] that the King came to be chosen from within the same family, and only with Hugh Capet[13] that the principle of primogeniture was adopted. In Scandinavia, the King was elected by a provincial *thing*, and his election had then to be confirmed by other assemblies across the country. Among other Germanic peoples, the practice of 'shielding'[14] is recorded.[15] The Emperor of the Holy Roman Empire also was elected, and the importance of the Prince-Electors in German history[16] is well known. In general, it is only from the Twelfth century onwards that elective monarchies all around Europe became hereditary. Until the French

---

9   'Le pouvoir des idées en démocratie', in *Pouvoirs*, May 1983, p. 145.

10 Publius Cornelius Tacitus (56 CE?-117 CE?) was a Roman Senator and historian who wrote a number of works, including one of the earliest accounts of the Germanic tribes, *Germania*. (Ed.)

11 Tacitus, *The Agricola and The Germania* (New York: Penguin Books, 1970), p. 107.

12 Pippin, or Pepin, was the first King of the Franks, as well as the founder of the Carolingian dynasty which deposed the Merovingians for rule of the kingdom. He ruled as King of the Franks from 751 until 768 CE. The Carolingians asserted their right to hereditary rule, although they were never successful in ending the traditional practice of electoral monarchy. (Ed.)

13 Hugh Capet (939?-996) was elected as the first King of France and was the founder of the Capetian dynasty. All French kings who came after him until the end of the French monarchy were part of the Capetian dynasty. (Ed.)

14 'Shielding' was the practice of raising the new King onto his soldiers' shields. (Ed.)

15 Significantly, it was following an inquiry into the origins of the Frankish royalty that nobles under Louis XIV reacted against the monarchic principle.

16 The Prince-Electors were those in the Holy Roman Empire who selected the Emperor. (Ed.)

Revolution, kings nevertheless continued to rule with the aid of parliaments, whose power was far from negligible. In all ancient European communities, one's status as a freeman brought political rights. 'Citizens' were organised in free popular communes, which, among other things, possessed municipal charters. Sovereigns were surrounded by councils with which they would make decisions. The influence of customary law on juridical practices is itself an index of the degree of popular 'participation' in the drafting of laws. In other words, the old monarchies cannot be said to have lacked popular legitimacy.

The oldest parliament in the Western world, the Icelandic Althing, was established in the year 930. It consists of a federal assembly whose members meet each year in the inspired setting of Thingsvellir. Adam of Bremen wrote, around 1076, that 'among them there is no king, but only law'.[17] The *thing*, or local parliament, refers to both a place and an assembly in which freemen possessing equal political rights met at appointed dates to legislate and deliver justice.[18] In Iceland, every freeman enjoyed two inalienable rights: to bear arms and to take a seat at the *thing*. The Icelanders, Frédéric Durand writes, 'managed to set up and run what, by using a vague but suggestive analogy, may be termed a sort of Nordic Hellas, a community of free citizens who took an active part in the affairs of their community—surprisingly cultured and intellectually productive men united by bonds of mutual esteem and respect.'[19]

'Scandinavian democracy is very old: its origins can be traced back to the traditions of the Viking era', Maurice Gravier observes.[20] Throughout northern Europe, this 'democratic' tradition rests on a particularly strong communitarian sentiment—a tendency towards *zusammenleben* ('living together') which leads people to take account of common interests above all else. At the same time, this democracy

---

17 Adam of Bremen, *History of the Archbishops of Hamburg-Bremen* (New York: Columbia University Press, 1959), p. 217. (Ed.)

18 The word *thing*, which describes the parliament, stems from a Germanic term originally meaning 'that which comes together'. The word is cognate to the Old English 'thing' (German 'Ding'). The term would appear to have initially described the assembly in which public matters were discussed, then public affairs in general, and finally the 'things' discussed.

19 'Les fondements de l'État libre d'Islande: trois siècles de démocratie mediévale', in *Nouvelle École* 25-26, Winter 1974-75, pp. 68-73.

20 Maurice Gravier, *Les Scandinaves* (Paris: Lidis-Brépols, 1984), p. 613.

is tinged with a clear sense of hierarchy, which justifies the use of the expression 'aristo-democracy'. This tradition, founded on mutual assistance and a feeling of shared responsibility, remains alive in many countries, starting with Switzerland.

The idea that the people are the original possessors of power surfaces again and again in the history of the Middle Ages. While the clergy limited itself to proclaiming that *omnis potestas a Deo* (all power comes from God), certain theorists argued that power only flows to the sovereign from God through the intercession of the people. The notion of 'power by divine right' was thus assumed in an indirect way, without turning the people into an abstraction. Marsilius of Padua[21] did not hesitate to proclaim the concept of popular sovereignty; significantly, he did so to defend the supremacy of the Emperor (at the time, Ludwig of Bavaria) over the Church. The idea of a lack of distinction in principle between the people and their leaders is again attested by the formula *populus et proceres* ('the people and the great ones'), which occurs again and again in ancient texts.

One should mention here the democratic tendencies found in Rome,[22] as well as in the ancient Italian republics, in French and Flemish communes, in Hanseatic municipalities,[23] and in the constitutional charters of the free Swiss cantons. We should further recall the ancient *boerenvrijheid* ('farmers' freedom') that prevailed in the Frisian provinces during the Middle Ages and whose equivalent could be found along the North Sea, in the Low Countries, Flanders, Scandinavia, Germany, Austria, and Switzerland. Finally, it is worth mentioning the existence of important communal movements based on guilds and franchises, which fought for mutual support and pursued economic and political goals. At times, these clashed with royal authority and the Church, with the support of the burgeoning bourgeoisie, while at

---

21 Marsilius of Padua (1275?-1342?) was a scholar in Fourteenth century Italy. His best-known work is *Defensor pacis* (*The Defender of Peace*), in which he called for a separation between the authority of the Emperor and the Pope in the Holy Roman Empire, seeking to limit the powers of the Papacy. One of his prescriptions was that the Pope should be an elected position. (Ed.)

22 See P. M. Martin, *L'idée de royauté à Rome. De la Rome royale au consensus républicain* (Clermont-Ferrand: Adosa, 1983).

23 The Hanseatic League was an economic bloc formed by many northern European cities between the Thirteenth and Seventeenth centuries. (Ed.)

others they backed the monarchy in its fight against the feudal lords and contributed to the rise of the mercantile bourgeoisie.[24]

The vast majority of political regimes throughout history can actually be classed as mixed. 'All ancient democracies', François Perroux observed, 'were governed by a *de jure* or *de facto* aristocracy, when they were not ruled by a monarchical principle.'[25] According to Aristotle, Solon's constitution[26] was oligarchic for the Areopagus,[27] aristocratic for its magistrates, and democratic for the make-up of its tribunals. Hence, he added, it combined the advantages of all forms of government. Similarly, according to Polybius,[28] Rome was an elective monarchy in terms of the power of its consuls, an aristocracy in terms of the power of the Senate, and a democracy in terms of the rights of the people. Cicero,[29] in his *On the Republic*, adopts a similar perspec-

---

24 'Democracy', both in this case and in relation to the free peasantry, already featured social demands, although not 'class struggle' (a concept clearly not found among ancient democracies). In the Middle Ages these demands essentially aimed at giving a voice to those who were excluded from power. Yet 'democracy' could also be used against the people. In Medieval Florence, social strife between the '*popolo grosso*' (the wealthy merchants-Ed.) and the '*popolo minuto*' (literally 'little people', or shopkeepers-Ed.) was particularly rampant. On this Francesco Nitti writes, 'The reason why the working classes in Florence proved lukewarm in the defence of their liberty and sympathised with the Medici was because they were opposed to democracy, which—as we would say—was an ideal cherished by the rich bourgeoisie' (Francesco Nitti, *La démocratie*, vol. 1 [Paris: Félix Alcan, 1933], p. 57).

25 This opinion is shared by most of those who have studied ancient democracies. Victor Ehrenberg—to mention only one example—sees Greek democracy as a 'kind of extended aristocracy' (*The Greek State* [London: Methuen, 1969], p. 50).

26 Solon was an Athenian lawmaker in the Sixth century BCE who drafted a constitution to make the state more resistant to tyranny. According to Aristotle, who wrote about Solon in his *Politics*, Solon sought to admit all citizens to the parliament and the court, and his constitution divided Athens into four social classes based upon property ownership. Various levels of access to the government were granted to each of the top three classes, although the fourth class was completely excluded. (Ed.)

27 The council of elders of ancient Athens. (Ed.)

28 Polybius was an Arcadian historian of the Second century BCE, and author of *The Histories*. He lived in Rome and studied the form of government of the Republic. He developed the idea of separation of powers between the branches of government which were later influential upon Cicero, Montesquieu and the U.S. Constitution. (Ed.)

29 Marcus Tullius Cicero (106-43 BCE) was a philosopher and famed orator in the Roman Republic who introduced many Greek concepts into Roman culture. (Ed.)

tive. Monarchy need not exclude democracy, as is shown for instance by contemporary constitutional and parliamentary monarchies. In 1789 it was, after all, the French monarchy which established the Estates-General. 'Democracy, taken in the broad sense', Pope Pius XII observed, 'admits of various forms, and can be realised in monarchies as well as in republics'.[30]

Let us further add that the experience of modern times shows that neither the political regime of a country nor its institutions necessarily constitute decisive factors in shaping the social life of its citizens. Comparable types of government may correspond to very different types of societies, whereas different forms of government may conceal identical social realities. (Western society today has an extremely homogeneous structure, although the institutions and constitutions of the countries it includes sometimes differ substantially.)

The task of defining democracy now appears even more difficult. The etymological approach is misleading. According to its original meaning, democracy means 'the power of the people'. Yet, this power can be interpreted in very different ways. The most reasonable approach, then, appears to be the historical one, which begins with the premise that 'genuine' democracy is first of all the political system established in Antiquity by those who invented both the thing itself and the word that describes it.

The notion of democracy never occurred at all in modern political thought before the Eighteenth century. Even then, it was only sporadically mentioned, and usually with a pejorative connotation. Until the French Revolution, the most 'advanced' philosophers fantasised about mixed regimes combining the advantages of an 'enlightened' monarchy with those of popular representation. Montesquieu[31] acknowledged the people's right to monitor, but not to govern. Not a single revolutionary constitution claimed to have been inspired by 'democratic' principles. Robespierre[32] is one of the few figures of his time who—towards the

---

30 From 'Democracy and a Lasting Peace', 1944 Christmas Message, available at www.papalencyclicals.net/Pius12/P12XMAS.HTM. Accessed 5 November 2010. (Ed.)

31 Charles de Secondat, Baron de Montesquieu (1689-1755) was a French Enlightenment philosopher who is best-known for *The Spirit of the Laws*, which is a fundamental work in the development of modern democratic ideology. (Ed.)

32 Maximilien François Marie Isidore de Robespierre (1758-1794) was the most powerful member of the notorious Committee of Public Safety during the French

end of his reign—explicitly invoked democracy (something which did not contribute to strengthen his popularity in subsequent years). This regime he envisaged as a representative form of government: as 'a state in which the sovereign people, guided by laws which are of their own making, do for themselves all that they can do well, and, by their delegates, do all that they cannot do for themselves'.[33]

It was only in the United States, once people had started criticising the notion of a 'republic', that the word democracy first became widespread. Its usage became current at the beginning of the Nineteenth century, especially with the advent of Jacksonian democracy and the establishment of the Democratic Party. The word then crossed the Atlantic again and became firmly implanted in Europe in the first half of the Nineteenth century. Tocqueville's[34] essay *Democracy in America*, which elicited considerable success, made the term a household word.

Despite the many quotes inspired by Antiquity that adorn the speeches of Eighteenth century philosophers and politicians, the genuine political inspiration drawn from ancient democracy was very weak at that time. The philosophers admired Sparta more than Athens, and the 'Sparta vs. Athens' debate—often distorted by bias or ignorance—pitted the partisans of authoritarian egalitarianism against the tenets of moderate liberalism.[35] Rousseau,[36] for instance, who abhorred

---

Revolution, which ordered many executions that came to be known as the Reign of Terror. In spite of his insistence that he was serving the interests of the people, his excesses eventually led to his own execution. (Ed.)

33   Address given on 5 February 1794, reprinted in Keith Michael Baker, *The Old Regime and the French Revolution* (Oxford: Pergamon Press, 1987), p. 371.

34   Alexis de Tocqueville (1805-1859) was a French political thinker best known for his work, *Democracy in America,* which was based on his experiences while travelling in the U.S. Although Tocqueville was a classical liberal who opposed the monarchy of his day, he also opposed the socialist radicals. In his study of the U.S., he praised America's democratic system, but disliked Americans' obsession with money and their contempt for elites, since even though the latter is what enabled them to do away with the old colonial aristocracy, it also caused them to disregard the most intelligent members of their society, coining the term 'tyranny of the majority' to describe it. (Ed.)

35   On this debate, see in particular Luciano Guerci's work *Libertà degli antichi e libertà dei moderni: Sparta, Atene e i 'philosophes' nella Francia del settecento* (Naples: Guida, 1979).

36   Jean-Jacques Rousseau (1712-1778) was a philosopher whose republican philosophy was highly influential upon the ideals of the French Revolution. (Ed.)

Athens, expressed sentiments that were rigorously philo-Laconian, which is to say pro-Spartan. In his eyes, Sparta was first and foremost the city of equals (*homoioi*). In contrast, when Camille Desmoulins[37] thundered against Sparta, it was to denounce its excessive egalitarianism: against the Girondist Brissot,[38] he attacked Lycurgus,[39] 'who made his citizens equal just as a tornado renders equal all whom it has struck'. All in all, it remained a rather superficial discourse. The cult of Antiquity chiefly functioned as a metaphor for regeneration, as exemplified by the words Saint-Just[40] hurled at the Convention:[41] 'The world has been empty since the Romans; their memory can replenish it and augur liberty again!' (11 Germinal, year 2).[42]

In order to study 'genuine' democracy, it is necessary to turn to Greek democracy rather than to those regimes that the contemporary world wishes to describe by this term.

The comparison between ancient and modern democracies is a common academic exercise.[43] It is generally emphasised that the for-

---

37 Camille Desmoulins (1760-1794) was a journalist who was an important supporter of the French Revolution. He was later executed on the order of Robespierre. (Ed.)

38 Jacques Brissot (1754-1793) was a revolutionary thinker of the French Revolution and an admirer of the early United States. He was the most prominent member of the Girondists, which was an intellectual current, associated with Jacobinism, which favoured more radical egalitarianism and foreign policy. However, he opposed the excesses of the Reign of Terror, and he and many of the Girondists were eventually among its victims. (Ed.)

39 Lycurgus was a lawmaker in Eighth century BCE Sparta who established the institutions which came to define it. (Ed.)

40 Louis Antoine de Saint-Just (1767-1794) was a French revolutionary who was closely associated with Robespierre and the Reign of Terror. He was executed at the same time as Robespierre. (Ed.)

41 The National Convention was the revolutionary legislative body of France between 1792 and 1795. (Ed.)

42 It is striking that in the contemporary age it is Athens that has won the favour of democrats, with Sparta being denounced for its 'warrior spirit'. This change in discourse deserves detailed analysis. (The new Republican government during the French Revolution instituted the Republican Calendar as part of their larger effort to remove all traces of the old society from France. It was used between 1793 and 1805. Germinal was the seventh month of the calendar, corresponding to late March and early April.-Ed.)

43 See, for instance, Moses I. Finley's book *Democracy Ancient and Modern* (New Brunswick: Rutgers University Press, 1973), which is both a highly erudite study

mer were direct democracies, whereas the latter (for reasons that have to do, it is said, with their territorial extension and the size of their population) are representative democracies. We are also reminded of the fact that slaves were excluded from Athenian democracy, and hence that this regime was not so democratic after all. These two affirmations are rather simplistic.

Readied by the political and social evolution of the Sixth century BCE and the reforms carried out from the time of Solon, Athenian democracy met its founding moment with the reforms of Cleisthenes,[44] who returned from exile in 508 BCE. Firmly established in 460 BCE, it thrived for one and a half centuries. Pericles,[45] who succeeded Ephialtes in 461 BCE, gave democracy an extraordinary reputation, not without exercising a quasi-royal authority over the city for more than thirty years.[46]

The Greeks primarily defined democracy in contrast to two other systems: tyranny and aristocracy.[47] Democracy presupposed three conditions: *isonomy* (equality before the law), *isotimy* (equal rights to access all public offices), and *isegory* (freedom of expression). This was direct democracy, also known as 'face to face' democracy, since all citizens could take part in the *ekklesia*, or assembly. Deliberations were prepared by the *boule* (council), but it was the popular assembly that was the real decision-making body. The assembly appointed ambassadors, decided over the issue of war and peace, launched and brought

---

and a treatise of great contemporary relevance. In its French edition (Paris: Payot, 1976), it includes a long preface by Pierre Vidal-Naquet, who—among other errors—attributes to Julien Freund views which are exactly the opposite of those held by him (see Freund's reply in 'Les démocrates ombrageux', *Contrepoint, art. cit.*).

44 Cleisthenes is credited with making democratic reforms in Athenian society in approximately 508 BCE, and is often called 'the father of Athenian democracy'. (Ed.)

45 Pericles (495?-429 BCE) governed Athens during its 'Golden Age' between the Persian and Peloponnesian Wars, when Athens made many of its greatest achievements. He also introduced many democratic reforms. (Ed.)

46 To quote Thucydides, 'He [i.e., Pericles], influential through both reputation and judgment and notable for being most resistant to bribery, exercised free control over the people ... he did not speak to please in order to acquire power by improper means ... And what was in name a democracy became in actuality rule by the first man' (*History of the Peloponnesian War*, Book Two, text 65).

47 One of the best works on the matter is Jacqueline de Romilly's *Problèmes de la démocratie grecque* (Paris: Hermann, 1975).

an end to military expeditions, investigated magistrates' performance, issued decrees, ratified laws, bestowed citizenship rights, and deliberated on matters of public security. In short, 'the people ruled, instead of being ruled by elected individuals', as Jacqueline de Romilly writes, quoting the text of the oath given by the Athenians: 'I will kill whoever by word, deed, vote, or hand attempts to destroy democracy ... And should somebody else kill him, I will hold him in high esteem before the gods and divine powers, as if he had killed a public enemy.'

Democracy in Athens primarily meant a community of *citizens*, which is to say the community of the people of Athens gathered in the *ekklesia*. Citizens were classified according to their membership in a *deme*, a grouping simultaneously territorial, social, and administrative. The very term *demos*, which is of Doric[48] origin, designates those who live in a given territory, as well as the territory itself as a place of origin determining civic status—inextricably linking the two.[49] To some extent, *demos* and *ethnos* coincide: democracy is conceived here in relation not to the individual, but to the *polis*, which is to say the city as an *organised community*. Slaves were excluded from voting not because they were slaves, but because they were non-citizens. We seem shocked by this today. But what democracy has ever accorded suffrage to non-citizens?[50]

The notions of citizenship, liberty, and equality of political rights, as well as popular sovereignty, were closely interrelated. The most essential feature of citizenship was one's origin and heritage: Pericles was the 'son of Xanthippus from the *deme* of Cholargus'. From 451 BCE, one had to be born of an Athenian mother and father in order to become a citizen. Defined by his belonging, the citizen (*polites*) was opposed to the *idiotes*, or non-citizen—a designation that quickly took on a pejorative meaning (from the notion of the isolated individual with no belonging came the idea of the 'idiot'). Citizenship as a function thus

---

48 The Dorians were one of the four tribes of ancient Greece. The Spartans were Doric. (Ed.)

49 The word *demos* is opposed in this respect to *laos*, another term that was used in Greece to describe the people, but with the express meaning of 'community of warriors'.

50 In France—to mention only one example—the right to vote was only gradually implemented. In 1791 a distinction was still being drawn between 'active' and 'passive' citizens. Subsequently, suffrage was extended to all taxpayers. The universal suffrage proclaimed in 1848 remained limited to males until 1945.

derived from the notion of citizenship a status which was the exclusive prerogative of birth. To be a citizen meant, in the fullest sense of the word, to belong to a homeland—that is, to a homeland and a past. One is born an Athenian—one does not become it (rare exceptions notwithstanding). Besides, the Athenian tradition discouraged mixed marriages. Political equality, established by law, derived from a common origin, which it also sanctioned. Only birth conferred individual *politeia*.[51] Democracy was rooted in a notion of *autochthonous*[52] citizenship, which intimately linked its exercise to the origins of those who exercised it. Fifth century BCE Athenians constantly celebrated themselves as 'the autochthonous people of great Athens', and it was upon this founding myth that they based their democracy.[53]

In Greek, just as in Latin, liberty stems from one's origin. Freeman, **(e)leudheros* (Greek *eleutheros*), is primarily he who belongs to a certain 'stock' (cf. the Latin word *liberi*, 'children'). 'To be born of good stock is to be free', Émile Benveniste writes, 'it comes to the same thing.'[54] Similarly, in Germanic, the kinship between the words *frei*, 'free', and *Freund*, 'friend', shows that originally freedom sanctioned a mutual belonging. The Indo-European root **leudh-*, from which both the Latin *liber* and the Greek *eleutheros* are derived, also served to designate 'people' as belonging to a given folk (cf. the Old Slavonic *ljudú*, 'folk', and German *leute*, 'people'). These terms all derive from a root evoking the idea of 'growth and development'.

The original meaning of the word 'liberty' in no way suggests the idea of 'liberation' as emancipation from a given community. Rather, it implies a form of *belonging*—and it is this which confers liberty. Hence, when the Greeks spoke of liberty, it is not the right to escape

---

51 On the evolution of this notion, see Jacqueline Bordes, '*Politeia*' dans la pensée grecque jusqu'à Aristote (Paris: Belles Lettres, 1982).

52 Autochthonous is a concept emphasising the relationship between the citizens of a nation and the land in which they are born. (Ed.)

53 Nicole Loraux, in The Children of Athena: Athenian Ideas about Citizenship and the Division between the Sexes (Princeton: Princeton University Press, 1993), has interpreted the Athenian notion of citizenship as the 'ideal of the autochthonous'. The myth of Erichthonios (or Erechtheus) explains the autochthonous character and the origins of male democracy, while rooting the Athenian ideology of citizenship in timeless foundations.

54 Émile Benveniste, Indo-European Language and Society (Coral Gables: University of Miami Press, 1973), p. 262.

the tutelage of the city that they had in mind or the right to rid themselves of the constraints to which each citizen was bound. Rather, what they had in mind was the right—and *political capability*—guaranteed by law of *participating* in the life of the city, voting in the assembly, electing magistrates, etc. Liberty did not legitimise secession, but sanctioned its very opposite: the bond which tied each person to his city. This was not *liberty as autonomy*, but *liberty as participation*. It was not meant to extend beyond the community, but was practised solely within the framework of the *polis*. Liberty implied belonging. The 'liberty' of an individual lacking any form of belonging, i.e., a *deracinated* individual, was completely devoid of any meaning.

If it is thus true that liberty was directly linked to the notion of democracy, then it must also be added that liberty meant first and foremost the *liberty of the people*, from which the liberty of citizens follows. In other words, it is the liberty of the people (or of the city) that *lays the foundations* for the equality of individual political rights, which is to say the rights enjoyed by individuals as citizens. Liberty presupposes *independence* as its primary condition. Man lives in society, and therefore individual liberty cannot exist without collective liberty. Among the Greeks, individuals were free because (and insofar as) their city was free.

When Aristotle defines man as a 'political animal' and a *social* being, when he claims that the city precedes the individual and that only within society can the individual achieve his potential,[55] what he is suggesting is that man should not be detached from his role as a citizen—as a person living in an organised community, a *polis* or *civitas*. This view stands in contrast to the concept of modern liberalism, which assumes that the individual precedes society and that man, *qua* individual, is *at once* something more than just a citizen.[56]

In a 'community of freemen', then, individual interests must never prevail over common interests. 'All those governments which have a common good in view', Aristotle writes, 'are rightly established and strictly just, but those who have in view only the good of the rulers

---

55 Aristotle, *Politics*, 1253a, 19–20.

56 On the work of Aristotle and his relationship with the Athenian constitution, see James Day and Mortimer Chambers, *Aristotle's History of Athenian Democracy* (Berkeley: University of California Press, 1962).

are all founded on wrong principles'.[57] In contrast to what we find in Euripides,[58] for instance, in Aeschylus[59] the city is regularly described as a unit. 'It was that sense of community', Moses I. Finley writes, 'fortified by the state religion, by their myths and their traditions, which was an essential element in the pragmatic success of Athenian democracy'.[60]

In Greece, Finley adds, 'freedom meant the rule of law and participation in the decision-making process, not the possession of inalienable rights'.[61] The *law* merged, in practice, with the genius of the city. 'To obey the law meant to be devoted with zeal to the will of the community', Paul Veyne observes.[62] It is liberty that brings legality: *Legum servi sumus ut liberi esse possimus*, as Cicero put it.[63]

By showing that the fundamental principle of democracy is liberty,[64] Aristotle intends to emphasise that it is not equality. Among the Greeks, equality was only a *means* to democracy, not its cause. Political equality derived from citizenship—from one's belonging to a given people. The underlying assumption here is that members of the same people (or city), whatever their mutual differences, are all citizens in the same way. This equality of rights by no means reflects a belief in *natural* equality. The equal right of all citizens to take part in the assembly does not imply that men are equal (or that it would be preferable if they were), but rather that from their common belonging to the city they derive a common capacity to exercise the right of

---

57 Aristotle, *Politics*, 1279a, 17sq. This specific translation is taken from *The Politics and Economics of Aristotle* (London: Henry G. Bohn, 1853), p. 94. (Ed.)

58 Euripides (480 BCE?-406 BCE) was one of the great Athenian tragic playwrights. (Ed.)

59 Aeschylus (524 BCE?-455 BCE?) was the first of the great Athenian tragic playwrights. (Ed.)

60 Moses I. Finley, *Democracy Ancient and Modern* (New Brunswick: Rutgers University Press, 1973), p. 29.

61 *Ibid.*, p. 116.

62 'Les Grecs ont-ils connu la démocratie?', *Diogène*, October-December 1983, p. 9. Paul Veyne adds, 'Bourgeois liberalism organises cruise ships in which each passenger must take care of himself as best he can, as the crew is only there to provide common goods and services. The Greek city, in contrast, was a ship where the passengers made up the crew'.

63 'We are all servants of the laws, for the very purpose of being able to be freemen', in *Oration for Aulus Cuentius Habitus*, chapter 53, in *The Orations of Marcus Tullius Cicero*, vol. 2 (London: Henry G. Bohn, 1852), p. 164. (Ed.)

64 In Aristotle, *Politics*, Book 7, Chapter 1.

suffrage, which is the privilege of citizens. As the appropriate means to the *techne* (skill) of politics, equality remains exterior to man. It simply represents the logical consequence of a shared belonging, as well as the primary condition for common participation. In the eyes of the Greeks, it was right for all citizens to engage in the political life not by virtue of universal and inalienable rights possessed by each human as such, but by virtue of their citizenship. Ultimately, the crucial notion here is not equality but citizenship. Greek democracy is that form of government in which the liberty of each citizen is *founded* on an equality conferred by the law, enabling him to enjoy civic and political rights.

The study of ancient democracy has elicited a range of reactions from modern authors. For some, Athenian democracy is an admirable example of civic responsibility (Francesco Nitti); for others it evokes the realm of 'activist' political parties (Paul Veyne);[65] for others still, it is essentially totalitarian (Giovanni Sartori). In general, everyone agrees that considerable differences exist between ancient and modern democracy. Curiously, however, it is modern democracies that are used as a criterion to measure the democratic consistency of the former. This is a rather odd way of reasoning. As previously noted, it was only belatedly that the modern political regimes which are described as 'democracies' today came to identify themselves as such. At a later stage, observers began inquiring into ancient democracies, and once they realised that they differed from the modern, they drew the conclusion that they must have been 'less democratic' than ours. But really, should we not proceed through the opposite kind of reasoning? Democracy was born in Athens in the Fifth century BCE. Hence, it is Athenian democracy (regardless of how we wish to judge it) that constitutes 'genuine' democracy. If contemporary democratic regimes differ from Athenian democracy, then they differ from democracy as such. Clearly, this is what irks most of our contemporaries. Since nowadays everyone wishes to cast himself as a democrat, and in the most accomplished possible way, and given the fact that Greek democracy hardly resembles the democracies before our eyes, it is naturally the Greeks who must be 'less democratic' than us. We thus reach the paradoxical conclusion that ancient democ-

---

65 For a 'liberal' critique of Greek democracy, see Paul Veyne, *art. cit.*, and Giovanni Sartori, *op. cit.*

racies, in which the people participated directly in the exercise of power, are disqualified on the grounds that they do not fit the standards of modern democracies, in which the people, at best, exercise only a very indirect control.

There should be no doubt that ancient and modern democracies are two entirely different systems. The very parallel drawn between them is misleading. All these systems have in common is their name, for they are the result of completely different historical processes.

Wherein do these differences lie? It would be wrong to assume that they only have to do with the 'direct' or 'indirect' nature of the decision-making process. Rather, they are due to two different conceptions of man, two different views of the world and of social ties. Ancient democracy was communitarian and 'holistic', whereas modern democracy is primarily individualistic. Ancient democracy defined citizenship by one's origin, and gave citizens the opportunity to participate in the life of the city. Modern democracy organises atomised individuals into citizens, primarily viewing them through the lens of abstract egalitarianism. Ancient democracy was based on the idea of organic community; modern democracy, as an heir to Christianity and the philosophy of the Enlightenment, on the individual. The meaning of the words 'city', 'people', 'nation' and 'liberty' radically changes from one model to the other.

In this respect, to argue that Greek democracy was only a direct democracy because it encompassed a small number of citizens is again rather simplistic. Direct democracy need not be associated with a limited number of citizens. It is rather primarily associated with a relatively homogeneous people conscious of what makes it such. The effective functioning of Greek democracy, as well as of Icelandic democracy, was first and foremost the result of cultural cohesion and a clear sense of shared belonging. The closer the members of a community are to one another, the more likely they are to have common sentiments, identical values, and the same way of viewing the world and social ties, and the easier it is for them to make collective decisions concerning the common good without the need for any form of mediation. Modern societies, in contrast, require a range of *intermediaries*, as they have ceased to be places of collectively lived *meaning*. The aspirations expressed in these democracies spring from contradictory value systems that can no longer be reconciled through any unified decision. Since Benjamin Constant,[66] it has been possible to measure the extent to which the notion of liberty has changed under the influence of the individualistic egalitarian ideology. Returning to a Greek concept of democracy, therefore, does not mean nurturing the constantly frustrated hope of 'face to face' social *transparency*. Rather, it means re-appropriating—and adapting to the modern world—a notion of the people and of community that has been eclipsed by two thousand years of egalitarianism, rationalism and the exaltation of the rootless individual.

---

66 Henri-Benjamin Constant de Rebecque (1767-1830) was a French politician and political philosopher who was one of the first to apply the term 'liberal' to himself. He contrasted the democracy of the Ancients, which he described as directly participatory, with modern democracy, which was based on freedom from state intervention and law and, due to the larger size of modern societies, of necessity limited the participation of its citizens in the government through elected representatives. (In the original text, de Benoist here references 'The Liberty of Ancients Compared with that of the Moderns', 1816, available at www.earlymoderntexts.com/pdf/constant.pdf. Accessed 5 November 2010.) (Ed.)

II

A DEFENCE OF DEMOCRACY

De optimo statu: what is the best political system? This is a meaningless question. No political system exists that is preferable in itself in all historical epochs, circumstances and places. Likewise, no 'absolute' solution exists for human affairs, nor any 'ultimate way' of living for societies and peoples. To argue that the best form of government is that which best meets the interests of the people is simply to sidetrack the issue, for various and mutually contradictory ways of defining collective 'interest' exist (such as prosperity, happiness, power, and destiny). It may certainly be argued that the optimum system is that which gives the best *form* to the values of a given people. But this too is a rather vague answer. Depending on the historical period, needs will change. Requirements in times of peace will differ from requirements in times of war, and it is well known how unsuited the *État de droit*[1] is for facing necessities engendered by an 'emergency situation' (*Notfall*).

If we take the case of democracy, a question which soon presents itself is whether this system of government may be applicable throughout the world. Good reasons exist to doubt that this is the case. On the one hand, democracy—in the best sense of the term—is rooted in the institutional and political history of Europe. On the other, liberal democracy is intimately connected to Judaeo-Christian morality and the philosophy of the Enlightenment. In the name of what should

---

1   *État de droit* is a term that is an attempt to translate the German concept, originating with Kant, of the *Rechtsstaat* into French. The exact meaning of term is still debated, but it essentially means 'a state where the rule of law prevails'. (Ed.)

Third World countries be made to embrace this system? Once again, universality can here be seen to serve as an alibi for ethnocentrism.[2] The intrinsic 'goodness' of a political system cannot therefore be proven. At most, one may attempt to prove that a given form of government is *preferable* to another in given conditions and in order to reach a particular goal. Besides, all authors who have argued that democracy is the best of all systems have given up on the idea of establishing its intrinsic 'goodness' and have for the most part simply adopted a comparative approach: democracy—they argue—has certain flaws, but it has less flaws (or less serious flaws) than the other systems. This approach, however, regularly has to face the problem of the validity of its own postulates and criteria.[3] The simplest approach, therefore, is to accept that there is no ultimate or absolutely superior form of government and to measure the advantages and disadvantages of each system against the principles one has chosen to follow.

Democracy has been made the object of two sorts of criticism. The first is directed against the principle of democracy itself, and is generally of anti-democratic inspiration. The second, in contrast, consists of deploring the fact that democratic *practice* rarely conforms to the *ideal* or *theory* of democracy, and in suggesting possible solutions to

---

2 Peter L. Berger ('La démocratie dans le monde moderne', in *Dialogue* 2, 1984, pp. 2-6) has attempted to solve this dilemma by arguing that democracy derives its universality from the fact that it is the system most suited to the preservation of differences. Unfortunately, historical experience does not confirm this thesis. Berger, moreover, also points out that liberal democracy is based on a view of society whereby the individual is regarded as an 'autonomous being'; what he apparently does not realise is that in many Third World cultures the individual is not at all envisaged in these terms.

3 Giovanni Sartori (*op. cit.*), for instance, reckons that the most compelling argument in favour of democracy is the fact that it is open to change. Still, there is nothing to prove that the possibility of change is preferable to its impossibility. Moreover, the word 'change' is itself ambiguous. If by it one means that democracy is perfectible, this is a rather trivial assertion (for almost all political systems are perfectible). If instead one means that democracy may itself give way to a different regime, then it is difficult to see why democracy should initially be preferred. Similarly, the argument that democracy is to be preferred because it confers 'more freedom' presupposes agreement as to what we mean by this term; it also begs the question of why freedom should be given precedence over all other values. The argument that the democratic system is preferable because it reflects the feelings of the majority (something which in any case would have to be proven) begs the question of why we should wish to satisfy the will of the majority—and so on.

remedy the situation. History nonetheless shows that certain authors have adopted both forms of criticism at different stages. In this chapter we shall especially examine arguments of the first sort.

The principles of democracy have been criticised in the past both by Left wing and Right wing authors. In this respect, French revolutionary trade unionists from the 1896-1914 period, such as Georges Sorel, Édouard Berth, Pataud, Pouget, and Pelloutier, not unlike Proudhon and Blanqui, are closer than one would think to people such as Bonald, Joseph de Maistre, Maurras, Carlyle, and Spencer. Flaubert argued that universal suffrage is a 'disgrace to the human spirit';[4] Montalembert regarded it as a 'poison',[5] and Balzac as an 'utterly false principle'.[6] Auguste Comte claimed that popular sovereignty is a 'miserable lie'.[7] Renan proclaimed that voting fosters a 'destiny committed to the caprice of an average of opinion inferior to the grasp of the most mediocre sovereign called to the throne by the hazards of heredity'.[8] Countless other quotes could be added—each of these authors spawned a host of followers.[9]

Most of these criticisms are well known. According to their authors, democracy is the reign of division, instability, and incompetence *par excellence*—the dictatorship of numbers and mediocrity. The party system, it is argued, threatens national unity by engendering a state of 'endemic civil war'. Through electioneering and parliamentarianism, the most mediocre people come into power. As the number of those

---

4   From a letter by Flaubert to George Sand dated 8 September 1871, in Gustave Flaubert, *Selected Letters* (London: Penguin Books, 1997), p. 363. (Ed.)

5   Charles Forbes René de Montalembert (1810-1870) was a writer and Catholic Liberal who served in the Chamber of Deputies. In 1850 he supported a law restricting universal suffrage. (Ed.)

6   Honoré de Balzac (1799-1850) attacked universal suffrage in his novel *The Country Doctor*. (Ed.)

7   Auguste Comte (1798-1857) was one of the founders of positivism, and called for a new form of government based upon the principles of science. (Ed.)

8   Ernest Renan, *Recollections and Letters of Ernest Renan* (New York: Cassell, 1892), p. 175. (Ed.)

9   To refer to just a few relatively recent publications: Jean Haupt, *Le procès de la démocratie* (Chiré-en-Montreuil: Éditions de Chiré, 1977); Amédée d'Andigné, *L'équivoque démocratique* (Paris: Au Fil d'Ariane, 1963); Michel Fromentoux, *L'illusion démocratique* (Paris: NEL, 1975); Jean Madiran, *Les deux démocraties* (Paris: NEL, 1977). All these critiques, of traditionalist Catholic inspiration, are strikingly superficial and simplistic. (None of them have been translated.-Ed.)

taking part in the political process is higher in democracies, the game of politics becomes a mere clash between particular opposing interests. This in turn nourishes demagogy, making people lose sight of the general interest. As they must be re-elected, leaders are incapable of developing long-term projects and of taking necessary but unpopular steps. What they do, then, is encourage a range of groups to make claims that go against the common good; they speak the 'language of the masses' (Evola)[10] and, in order to satisfy the largest number of people, appeal to the lowest instincts. Democracy thus inevitably leads to anarchy, mass hedonism, and egalitarian materialism. The common good degenerates into the commonplace. The 'reign of freedom' reveals itself to be nothing but the reign of *quantity*. Democracy, as Maurras argued, 'consumes what previous ages have produced.'[11] The power of one man gives way to the dictatorship of all and to the tyranny of public opinion. The promotion of the 'average' individual causes a general levelling down. 'Democracy', Christian Perroux writes, 'draws everything down and makes it equal because equality and mass drawing down are part of its principles ... it is the rabble that makes the law.'[12]

Public opinion will often recognise that there is some truth to these criticisms,[13] but remains within the aforementioned *comparative* logic. It is thus noted that many criticisms directed against democracy *also* apply to other forms of government, for they concern unchanging traits of human nature. The prevalent feeling, in particular, is that democracy at least has the advantage of providing a safeguard against

---

10 Julius Evola (1898-1974) was the most important Italian member of the traditionalist school, which is to say that he opposed modernity in favour of an approach to life consistent with the teachings of the ancient sacred texts. De Benoist is likely referring to his book *Men Among the Ruins*, which is Evola's analysis of modern politics. (Ed.)

11 Charles Maurras (1868-1952) was a French Catholic counter-revolutionary philosopher who was the founder of the Action Française. His work is almost entirely untranslated. (Ed.)

12 Christian Perroux, *L'aurore, avenir du passé* (Paris: La Table ronde, 1984).

13 However, it generally regards these criticisms as being directed against extreme democratic claims rather than democracy itself. 'If it were not for the exaggerations of the perfectionist democrat, there would not be much material left to make up a case against democracy,' Giovanni Sartori writes in a book (*Democratic Theory*, pp. 52-53) that, despite its liberal bent, remains one of the best and most exhaustive works to have been published on the subject over the last twenty years.

despotism. Democratic regimes are defined in this context as regimes that *limit* power, as opposed to non-democratic forms of government, which are seen as regimes based on *unlimited authority*. Hence, giving up democracy would mean slipping into tyranny. Churchill famously stated that 'Democracy is the worst form of government except for all those other forms that have been tried from time to time'[14] (which allows Jean-Marie Le Pen,[15] among others, to call himself a 'Churchillian democrat'). The advantage of this formulation is that it avoids raising questions about *other* possible forms of democracy (not to mention other forms of government yet to be seen). Ultimately, what it says is that democracy may be a dreadful system, but the other systems are even more dreadful. Suddenly, democracy is no longer the 'best form of government', but only *the least bad.*

The 'democracy or dictatorship' dilemma is certainly striking. Yet, it is ill-founded: for the attainment of liberties has not always gone hand-in-hand with the extension of democracy. Besides, the vast majority of regimes in European history never denied the principle of liberty. As Tocqueville writes, 'Liberty has manifested itself to men in various times and forms. It is not associated exclusively with any social state, and one does not find it only in democracies. Hence it cannot constitute the distinctive characteristic of democratic centuries.'[16] This opinion is confirmed by Giovanni Sartori, who observes that, 'Our ideal of liberty does not intrinsically pertain to the development of the democratic ideal ... it is not a notion of democratic origin: it was acquired, not produced by democracy. There's a big difference.'[17]

Experience nevertheless shows—and this is a commonplace assertion—that democratic regimes can also be regimes of oppression, colonialism, and terror at times. 'Democracy, which is so beautiful in theory, can in practice lead to ghastly horrors', Alain[18] observed—and

---

14 Churchill said this at the House of Commons on 11 November 1947, as recorded in *Churchill by Himself* (London: Ebury, 2008), p. 574. (Ed.)

15 Le Pen was the founder and remains the leader of France's Far Right National Front party. Le Pen made this statement during a television appearance in 1984 and later claimed it as one of the pivotal moments of his career. (Ed.)

16 Alexis de Tocqueville, *Democracy in America* (New York: Library of America, 2004), p. 582. (Ed.)

17 *Op. cit.*

18 Alain was the pen name of Émile-Auguste Chartier (1868-1951), a famous French philosopher and pacifist. Several of his works have been translated. (Ed.)

his is but another way of saying that the road to hell is paved with good intentions. We all know what course the 'popular democracies' of eastern Europe took. Let us further recall that after proclaiming the 'rights of man', the French Revolution established the Reign of Terror and carried out the Vendean genocide.[19] As for the idea that universal suffrage leads to the disarming of extremists, as moderates always make up the majority of society, given all the evidence it underestimates the possible influence of social movements. Here too, illusions must be broken.

The opposition constantly emphasised, in liberal milieus, between democracy and totalitarianism also appears rather misleading. Several recent studies (such as those by J. L. Talmon[20] and Claude Polin[21]) have, in different ways, located the origins of modern totalitarianism within the context of the very ideology that has also spawned contemporary democracy, namely the egalitarianism and rationalism of the Enlightenment.[22] 'In the Eighteenth century', J. L. Talmon writes, 'at the same time as liberal democracy *and starting from the same premises*, a current developed that pushed towards what may be termed totalitarian democracy ... The two forms of democracy only branched off from the same tree after their shared beliefs were tested by the French Revolution'.[23] Finally, we should bear in mind that totalitari-

---

19 The Vendean genocide refers to an episode during the Reign of Terror when, in 1793, the citizens of the Vendée region of coastal France, who were supportive of both the clergy and the monarchy, began an uprising against the revolutionary Republican government. Following the defeat of the uprising in February 1794, the Committee of Public Safety ordered the Republican forces to conduct a scorched-earth razing of the area and the mass execution of its residents, including non-combatants, women and children. Several hundred thousand people are estimated to have been killed out of a population of 800,000. Some historians, especially on the Right, have classified this incident as a genocide, although this has been disputed. (Ed.)

20 J. L. Talmon, *The Origins of Totalitarian Democracy* (London: Secker & Warburg, vol. 1 1952, vol. 2 1960). (Ed.)

21 Claude Polin, *L'Esprit totalitaire* (Paris: Éditions du Sirey, 1977) and *Le totalitarisme* (Paris: Presses Universitaires de France, 1982).

22 See my article 'Un totalitarisme peut en cacher un autre', in *Éléments* 46, summer 1983, pp. 17-21.

23 From J. L. Talmon, *The Origins of Totalitarian Democracy, op. cit.* Perhaps it is in the light of this original shared heritage that we should explain the alliance during the last war between the USSR and the Western countries: for the Second World War—despite what is claimed on various sides—in no way witnessed an opposition between 'democracies' and totalitarianism. The opposition was rather

anism can take on different forms, and that the 'soft' standardisation we are starting to witness in liberal democracies today—a form of despotism that Tocqueville had already warned us about—is no less totalitarian than that which manifests itself through repression and concentration camps.[24]

We should face the facts: no democratic procedure can serve as an absolute guarantee against autocracy and despotism. A popular government, as Aristotle rightly noted, may become tyrannical. Dictatorship is not typical of monarchies or oligarchies. Rather, it represents a corruption that is always possible and which threatens—in different ways—all political systems.

Let us now return to modern criticisms of democracy. Ultimately, they may all be traced back to one specific criticism: the *law of numbers*. Jacqueline de Romilly sums it up nicely in just a few words: 'It may seem right for each person to contribute to the governing of a country through an equal vote; but it may also seem dangerous, as not everyone is equally competent. This, to put it simply, is the dilemma which every democracy faces'.[25] One consequence of the right to vote would certainly appear to be the fact that decisions are taken by the majority. Now, the idea that authority, a quality, may stem from numbers, a quantity, is rather disturbing.

It is on this very point that all criticisms of democracy centre. 'Ten million ignorant men cannot constitute a wise one',[26] Taine wrote in his Preface to *The Origins of Contemporary France* in 1876. A collection of errors does not make a truth: quality cannot stem from quan-

---

between two forms of totalitarianism, one of which—the Soviet—was supported by bourgeois democracies. This truly momentous alliance has for a long time vested 'liberal' sanction upon the Soviet camp, for the continuing benefit of international Communism.

24 Just as they draw an opposition between 'popular democracies' and 'liberal democracies', certain authors wish to contrast the American Revolution, which they claim was respectful of liberty, with the French Revolution, which brought about the Reign of Terror. This opposition, however, appears rather artificial. The American Revolution did not lead to the Reign of Terror because there was no local aristocracy it could suppress. In contrast, there was another group of people who held a certain 'precedence': the Indians. The massacre of the Indian tribes did not observe the principle of respect for 'human rights' any more than the followers of Monsieur Guillotin did.

25 *Problèmes de la démocratie grecque*, p. 19.

26 Hippolyte Taine, *The Ancient Régime* (New York: Henry Holt, 1876), p. vi. (Ed.)

tity—a value is not a weight. The reasons of the majority cannot be taken as *good reasons*. After all, why should the *most numerous* section of society *ipso facto* be considered the *best*? If we believe that the majority 'speaks the truth', are we not identifying the inclinations of the masses with a fanciful 'universal option'?

The above criticism immediately leads to another: not only does quantity not make quality, but indeed it often *unmakes* it. There appears to be a considerable risk, then, that the mathematical average on which universal suffrage is based may end up coinciding with the 'average' in the sense of the mediocre. It is then argued in this context that the 'best' are always a *minority*, and that the incompetence of leaders inevitably reflects that of the citizens who elected them. In his own day, Max Nordau[27] had already sought to 'scientifically' prove that the outcome of universal suffrage could only express the opinion of the mediocre. André Tardieu wrote, 'The law of numbers ends up bestowing power on incompetence ... The majority of voters are invited to make decisions regarding issues they know nothing about.'[28] René Guénon[29] proclaimed that the law of numbers is only the 'law of matter and brute force',[30] and that 'what is superior cannot stem from what is inferior'. He thus concluded, 'The opinion of the majority cannot be anything but an expression of incompetence.'[31] From another angle (for the aim here is to argue that the majority conceals the potential threat of tyranny), Bertrand de Jouvenel wrote, 'So far from massive majorities in favour of a government and its policy giving us a feeling of the excellence of a regime, they render it suspect to us.'[32]

---

27 Max Nordau (1849-1923) was a Hungarian Jew who moved to Paris and became a prominent conservative critic and Zionist. His best-known work is *Degeneration*, which is an all-out attack on modernity.

28 *Le souverain captif* (Paris: Flammarion, 1936).

29 René Guénon (1886-1951) was a French writer who founded what has come to be known as the traditionalist school of religious thought. Traditionalism calls for a rejection of the modern world and its philosophies in favour of a return to the spirituality and ways of living of the past. (Ed.)

30 René Guénon, *The Crisis of the Modern World* (Ghent, New York: Sophia Perennis, 2001), p. 76.

31 *Ibid.*, p. 75. See too *The Reign of Quantity and the Signs of the Times* (Ghent: Sophia Perennis, 2001).

32 Bertrand de Jouvenel, *Sovereignty: An Inquiry into the Political Good* (Chicago: University of Chicago Press, 1957), p. 276.

Along much the same lines, Tocqueville stated, 'I regard as impious and detestable the maxim that in matters of government the majority of a people has the right to do absolutely anything'.[33]

The keyword here is *competence*. The idea according to which the best government is comprised of 'those who know' stretches back to Antiquity. Also ancient is the notion that democracy operates a negative selection. Socrates himself, according to Plato, blamed the Athenians for discussing political matters 'without having learned and without having any teacher'.[34] Similarly, out of hostility toward the law of numbers, public opinion very frequently accepts the theory according to which procedures for political selection should primarily promote 'competent men' — an expression which in our age is increasingly being taken as a synonym for 'experts' and 'technicians'.

This stance in favour of 'competence' is ambiguous to say the least. First, no single definition of 'competence' exists, for competence can take many different forms. Most importantly, it is very dangerous to identify *competence* with *knowledge*, as anti-democratic critics almost invariably do. Max Weber[35] has shown what it is that makes the *scientist* different from the *politician*. The politician is not such because he possesses any specific form of 'knowledge', but because he is the one who must *decide* what goal knowledge should serve. The politician is not a *scientist* but a *decision-maker*. A statesman is not incompetent because he possesses little knowledge, but because he does not know how to draft a policy. The politician must no doubt surround himself with 'competent men' and 'technicians', if for no other reason than to entrust them with finding the *means* to implement his decisions (and in this respect, political action is not foreign to knowledge). But it is one thing to surround oneself with technicians and experts, and quite another to charge these people with identifying the objectives to be pursued. To wish to put the government into the hands of 'experts' is to forget the fact that the judgement of experts must itself be reassessed and re-evaluated, as political decision-making implies both conflicts of interest and a number of possible choices. Now, our age,

---

33 *Op. cit.*, p. 288. (Ed.)

34 Plato, *Protagoras*, 319d.

35 Max Weber (1864-1920) was a German who is considered one of the founders of sociology. His principal work is *The Protestant Ethic and the Spirit of Capitalism*. In this case, however, De Benoist is referring to Weber's two essays, *Politics as a Vocation* and *Science as a Vocation*. (Ed.)

which has previously bowed to the *myth* of decision-making via 'technical knowledge', is increasingly forgetful of all this. An acceptance of the *operative* role of experts may thus quickly lead to the legitimising of *technocracy*. Under the pretext that the increasing complexity of public affairs makes politics necessarily dependent upon 'those who know', the people are being stripped of their sovereignty, while the very notion of politics goes up in smoke.

From the standpoint of this overemphasis on 'competence', logic would have it that a financier should be appointed minister of finance, an economist minister of the economy, a teacher, minister of education, and so on. But this means forgetting that a 'technician minister' will tend to contribute only ideas deriving from his training and act exclusively in favour of the particular interests of his own professional category. More importantly, it means forgetting once more that knowledge in a given field does not in principle imply any competence to *develop a policy* in the sector in question. As Jacques Maritain[36] has noted, 'When a democracy breaks down, politics becomes the exclusive domain of an oligarchy of specialists.' This is all too true. Tocqueville was a remarkable observer of political systems. When appointed Minister for Foreign Affairs by Louis-Napoléon,[37] he accomplished the one act that most went against his own convictions: the launching of a military expedition to suppress the Roman Republic and re-establish the power of the Pope. Guizot,[38] another expert on the politics of his day, headed a cynical and shameless government. Many other more recent examples could be found.

The risk of the system degenerating is increased by the fact that technicians, by virtue of their training, cultivate the illusion that it is

---

36 Jacques Maritain (1882-1973) was a French Catholic philosopher who believed that Christian ethics were a necessary component of political systems. (Ed.)

37 Louis-Napoléon Bonaparte (1808-1873), as President of the Second Republic, sent troops into Italy in 1849 to restore the Pope as ruler of the Papal States after he had been overthrown by the republican revolt of Mazzini and Garibaldi. As a classical liberal, Tocqueville was sympathetic to the Republic's aims, and he believed that it was a mistake to fight the revolution when it was clear that it enjoyed a great deal of popular, nationalist support, even among the clergy. Bonaparte later became Napoleon III, Emperor of the Second French Empire. (Ed.)

38 François Pierre Guillaume Guizot (1787-1874) became Prime Minister of France in 1847. As a conservative, he supported many of the King's unpopular policies, such as restricting suffrage to an extremely small segment of the population. He was overthrown during the Revolution of 1848. (Ed.)

possible to rationally and 'objectively' determine not merely the means but also the objectives of political action. A discourse as relevant today as ever before, and which should be *read* as favouring the dispossession of politics by economics and technology, is that which speculates on the 'complexity of technological society' in order to turn government into a mere form of administration. At the same time, it is claimed that we should do away with 'ideological inertia'. Is it not revealing that economics and finance ministers are often appointed prime ministers? The underlying message here is that all objectives may ultimately be reduced to a single one. 'External constraints' and 'necessary rigour' are invoked to have us believe that, in this context, 'only one political approach is possible'; in other words, that *there is no choice*. Now, politics by definition is the art of making *choices*. In democracy, elections find their justification in the fact that voting allows citizens to express their preferences, i.e., to *choose*. But if 'there is no choice', then why vote? The very notion of elections thus loses its meaning. By promoting a *reductive* view of political and historical action, the myth of 'technical competence' proves profoundly undemocratic.

Is the criticism of democracy better founded when it stigmatises the 'incompetence' of voters? The opponents of democracy here appear to be confusing *generic* and *specific* competence. Now, what voters are asked for is not so much to be competent in choosing what must be done in a given field (after all, to make a similar request would be a waste of time), but rather to be *competent in discerning the difference between competence and incompetence*.

Does the electorate as a whole lack this 'generic' competence? It is easy to make such a claim. On the one hand, the desire to be *well governed* is no less legitimate and real than wanting to take part in the political process. The latter desire is always the means by which people think that the former may be pursued. Francesco Nitti argues, not without reason, that 'the public feeds on mediocrity, but does not love what is mediocre'.[39] The people never wish to be governed by 'men like the rest', men 'who are all alike'; rather, it wishes to be governed by men whom it has good reasons to respect and admire. Contrary to what is all too often claimed, voters do not wish the men they have elected to be in their image. Voters love greatness and are capable of recognising it. They love courage, even when they personally lack it. They may not

---

39 *La démocratie*, vol. 1.

know how to conduct a given policy, but can tell whether it suits them, just as they can appreciate a painting, or be art critics, even if they do not know how to paint, and enjoy a good book, even if they are not writers themselves. Aristotle, who was no partisan of egalitarianism, writes, 'The mass, while made up of individuals who, when considered in isolation, possess no great merits, may, once it comes together, prove superior to those who possess merits—this, not on an individual level, but as a collectivity'.[40] The question to be addressed, then, is what the specific competence of the people may be and in what sphere it can best be exercised.

The disgust which the political class elicits today is revealing. Very few citizens would be able to state precisely what it is that they do not like in politicians' actions and why they are less and less inclined to give them their trust. Still, citizens deep down *feel* that contemporary politicians do not meet their genuine aspirations. It is no exaggeration to think that the vast majority of citizens today—especially when they have a clear awareness of their shared belonging—are perfectly capable, if given the means to make a real choice (without being misled by propaganda and demagogy), of identifying the political acts most suited to the common good.

In this context, one should not underestimate the importance of the genuine phenomenon of *national and folk consciousness*, by means of which the collective representations of a desirable socio-political order are linked to a shared vision, comprised of a feeling of belonging that presents each person with imperatives transcending particular rivalries and tensions. In relation to this, Raymond Polin observes, 'The legitimacy of a government is not merely based on its respect for the constitution and the laws of the state and the laws and legal procedures that apply to the election of leaders .... The source of its legitimacy lies with the body of principles on which the deep-seated consensus of the nation is based. Founded upon history and reflected in its deeds and successes, it also expresses a vocation; it represents an appeal for deeds to come—the need to move on while preserving a sense of continuity. Resting on a given conception of man, of society and politics, this deep-seated consensus carries an obligation to build the future history of the nation according to the inspiration of

---

40 *Politics*, Book Three. (I cannot locate this passage in the text. The reference may be mistaken.-Ed.)

its spirit. Independently of the factors introduced by history, it pursues the creation of a culture marked by a unique spirit of its own: that of the nation ... It is this implicit philosophy, this living presence each member of a nation experiences through his own family milieu, circle of acquaintances, and culture, that constitutes the principle of national concord, which subsists in each person in a more profound and intimate way than his own explicit opinions; this concord is born out of the national spirit, out of the sense of belonging to a given culture, out of the love for one's country ... The legitimacy of political regimes and policies is thus based on a form of culture and a cultural mission ... Each national culture has a principle of legitimacy of its own, a specific mission it has entrusted to its own leaders in accordance with its own history and personality.'[41] The preservation of this national consciousness, and of the view that underlies it, appears today more than ever before as the chief prerequisite for the efficacy of democracy.

A distinction must also be drawn between voting which *decides* and voting which *appoints* (those who decide). Charles Maurras wrote, 'Will, decision-making and initiative all stem from small numbers; assent and acceptance from the majority.'[42] This is quite right. (Do contemporary democracies work any differently?) On the one hand, a people may completely identify itself with the will of its leaders—and it may be argued that it will do so insofar as it approves of this will and expresses no other. On the other hand, there are spheres in which a more *direct* form of competence may be exercised, as they concern things which individuals face in a more immediate manner. There is the problem of intermediary bodies, of professional or municipal life, of local democracy, and so on.

Another observation to be made is that anti-democratic criticism is curiously close to the liberal perspective, inasmuch as it implicitly embraces methodological individualism. A people, according to this view, is nothing but the sum of the individuals of which it is comprised: its overall 'incompetence' would simply follow from the incompetence of each single individual. This criticism actually does away with the very notion of a *people*. Of course, what it boils down to is a choice of

41 Raymond Polin and Claude Polin, *Le libéralisme, espoir ou péril* (Paris: La Table ronde, 1984), pp. 106-108.

42 Charles Maurras, *Enquête sur la monarchie* (Paris: Nouvelle Libr. nationale, 1909), p. 137.

values. It is possible to consider the people to be a negligible value. But if, on the contrary, it is taken as a fundamental category in the history of societies—as in our case—then one cannot escape the idea that the national and folk community ultimately constitutes the very source of political *legitimacy*. The notion of the people cannot be held as a central one while also rejecting all forms of democracy, which means 'power of the people'.

By our own understanding, a people is far more than just the sum of the individual characteristics possessed by each of its members. A people is an organic whole, possessing as such a distinct specificity. It differs from the *mass* insofar as it moves independently, with a life of its own. The mass is simply comprised of a transient plurality of isolated and rootless individuals. A people is instead a crucible by which citizens are *given form*. According to this 'holistic' perspective, democracy is a profoundly national vocation—at least when the people have the nation as its political form. Article 1 of the Constitution of the Weimar Republic proclaims, 'The power of the state comes from the people' (*die Staatsgewalt geht vom Volke aus*). On this basis, it may be argued that political power is legitimate when it meets the deepest aspirations of a people and enables everyone to contribute to its history. In the fullest sense of the term, democratic consciousness is the consciousness of a people when it puts itself to the test politically as such and seeks active expression in line with the consciousness it has of itself.

Now, not only are modern liberal democracies loathe to consider the people as an organic and relatively unitary notion, but the political practices they implement contribute to dismantle the people and divide it first into factions and parties, and then into individuals who are essentially alien to each another. The fact is that liberal democracies are rooted not so much in the spirit of ancient democracy as in Christian individualism, the rationalism of the Enlightenment, and the Anglo-Saxon Protestant spirit. In these democracies, the 'citizen' is not he who *inhabits* a history and destiny through his belonging to a given people, but rather an abstract, atemporal and universal being which, regardless of any belonging, is the holder of 'human rights' decreed to be inalienable. Man, exclusively defined by his ability to feel pleasure and pain, is merely 'what makes up the population', as Paul Veyne has written (coldly adding: 'in the sense in which statisticians will speak of a population of microbes or even of trees'). The individual person is here reduced to narcissistic subjectivity on the basis of a principle of equality. The notion of a people gives way to the vaguer one of 'society'. A liberal author such as Giovanni Sartori thus affirms that 'democracy is for politics what the market system is for economics'!

'Modern democracy', Francesco Nitti writes, 'is essentially American in its content and development'.[43] It may be argued, in this respect, that its extension goes hand-in-hand with that of the Anglo-Saxon spirit. It is little wonder, therefore, that liberal democracy does away with the notion of the people (Italian *popolo*, German *Volk*), since the English language does not even have a word to describe it.[44] The basis of modern 'American' democracy is both metaphysical and Christian. The Declaration of Independence of 1776 presents as 'self-evident truths' the ideas that 'all men are created equal' and that 'they are endowed by their Creator with certain unalienable rights'. Political equality here no longer derives from citizenship, but from the equal standing of all individual souls before their 'Creator'. 'Popular sovereignty' becomes a mere pretence: for it is actually subject to God's sovereignty.

It is thus easy to understand why the supporters of liberal democracy often express mistrust of the people, whose 'power' they nonetheless claim to acknowledge. 'The people creates nothing at all', Francesco Nitti proclaims, 'it merely gathers and preserves the efforts of isolated individuals'.[45] 'Power of the people' then merely serves as a *useful* formula. As Georges Burdeau has rightly explained, 'Revolutionary thought developed a notion of the people as committed to the protection of individual liberties. It was supported in this by the bourgeoisie, in whose interest it was to promote this notion of the people, as it would have helped assure its reign … Bourgeois thought, obsessed by the people—whose power it intuits—tends, or so it seems, to avert the threat it poses by drowning it in the abstraction of a concept which takes the edge off its dangerous nature'.[46]

---

43 *Op. cit.*, vol. 1.

44 The English word 'people', which is currently used to translate the French *peuple*, merely designates what in French would be *les gens*: an indeterminate plurality of individuals. Notions such as that of popular will, popular spirit, and popular soul are clearly inconceivable based on this word. (We have nevertheless been forced to use the word 'people' in this translation, for want of a better word.-Ed.)

45 *Op. cit.*, vol. 2, p. 124.

46 *La démocratie*, pp. 24-25.

Given these conditions, there is a considerable risk that in a liberal regime democratic life may no longer be identified with that of the people, and that 'the power of the people' may no longer describe the power held by the citizens of the country. René Capitant has most aptly noted that 'in an individualistic society, the idea of participation finds no space'.[47] According to liberalism, the individual comes before society and the latter is simply formed by individuals pursuing their own particular interests. This is an atomistic view of social life, which turns peoples and nations into transient superstructures that have little meaning. Now, Capitant continues, 'the development of democracy, conceived not merely as a form of state organisation, but also as a way of relating to others, is linked in contrast to the development of the realm of organised collective action. Society in this case is no longer seen as exclusively consisting of individuals, each pursuing his own private enterprise. Rather, society here assigns increasing importance to collective enterprises that bring men together through shared work and which are not simply the combination of individual efforts: for thanks to the specialisation of those involved and the merging of their wills, these enterprises take on an organic character.'[48]

The 'people's state', which is the genuine democratic state, should therefore not be confused with the liberal state. Democracy is first and foremost a '-cracy',[49] i.e., a form of power; as such, it implies authority. Liberalism is a doctrine concerned with the *limitation* of power and based on suspicion of authority. Democracy is a form of government and political action; liberalism, an ideology for the *restriction* of all government, which devalues politics in such a way as to make it dependent upon economics. Democracy is based on popular sovereignty; liberalism, on the rights of the individual.

Tocqueville, in the first volume of his work on American institutions, was the first to stress the difference between liberalism and democracy.[50] This distinction is particularly prominent in the history of French politics. While in Britain and in the United States democracy

---

47 René Capitant, *Démocratie et participation politique* (Paris: Bordas, 1972), p. 33.

48 *Ibid.*, p. 34.

49 The suffix '-cracy' by itself refers to any form of government. (Ed.)

50 In the second volume of his book, Tocqueville accused socialism, which was then starting to develop, of harbouring the same despotic tendencies he attributed to democracy.

was grafted upon liberalism, in France it is rather the opposite that occurred: we had Rousseau before Tocqueville and Benjamin Constant. This is the reason why the French political system remains an essentially mixed and, in certain respects, even contradictory one. Thus the Constitution of 1791 on the one hand proclaims, in the spirit of Rousseau, that 'the law is an expression of the general will' (Article 6); but on the other adds that 'all citizens have the right to contribute personally or via their representatives to its establishment'. Now, if the law is an expression of the general will, by definition it cannot be delegated. The allusion made here to 'representatives', which implies the delegation of sovereignty, stands in contradiction to what comes before.

In a recent work devoted to the 'republican ideology', Claude Nicolet has clearly illustrated the extent to which the French political tradition is removed from Anglo-Saxon liberalism. This tradition especially rejects the opposition drawn by Benjamin Constant between individual freedom and freedom as participation, as well as between civil and political society. 'The politics of the republicans', Nicolet writes, 'is of an ancient sort: politics as participation in power, even when—as under the Republic—this takes place via representatives. It is not politics as the limiting of power, as for Anglo-Saxons and liberals'.[51] As the jurist Carré de Malberg had already shown, the French political system is an *État légal*[52] rather than an *État de droit*: it tends to 'guarantee the supremacy of the legislative body and only entails the subordination of the administration to the laws', whereas the *État de droit* implies 'a system of limitations not only for the administrative authorities, but also for the legislative body'.[53]

* * *

We should now also focus on the 'anti-egalitarian' aspect of anti-democratic criticism. Certainly, it is quite right to see *equality* as the 'distinctly political concept' (Julien Freund) behind democracy. Yet we should agree on what this term means. In Greek democracy, as we

---

51 Claude Nicolet, *L'idée républicaine en France* (Paris: Gallimard, 1982), p. 357.

52 *État légal* roughly means 'state rule through democratically elected laws'. (Ed.)

53 R. Carré de Malberg, *Contribution à la théorie générale de l'État*, vol. 1 (Paris: CNRS, 1962), p. 492.

have seen, political equality was not seen to reflect any *natural* equality. Rather, it derived from citizenship and was but a means to freedom. All ancient authors who have extolled democracy have praised it not because it is an intrinsically egalitarian regime, but because it is a regime in which competition is open to all and enables a better selection of the elite. Plato, in his *Republic*, denounces those systems which dispense 'a sort of equality to both equals and unequals alike'.[54] Aristotle points out that justice also implies the idea of equality and inequality: 'Justice is thought by them to be, and is, equality; not, however, for whomever, but only for equals. And inequality is thought to be, and is, justice; neither is this for all, but only for unequals'.[55] Pericles himself, according to Thucydides, stressed that equality goes hand-in-hand with the systematic search for merits, which are by nature unequal.[56] Some modern authors have held much the same opinion: 'No intelligent person can believe that all men are equal', Francesco Nitti writes. He adds, 'Democracy does not mean equality among men, nor does it mean equality of wealth or of situations. Liberty enables all attitudes to find expression: as it is based on the equality of citizens before the law and in public offices, democracy inevitably engenders inequalities, which are necessary conditions for development in all advanced societies'.[57] Much in the same spirit, Giovanni Sartori argues that the aim of democracy is not to make individuals equal, but to *give them equal chances of being unequal*.

Actually, just as two ideas of liberty exist, there are also two ideas of equality. Isocrates[58] thus distinguishes between that equality which 'distributes the same to all' and that which gives 'each what he deserves',[59] condemning the former. Elsewhere, he writes that 'unequal merits will not lead to the same situations, and each one will be treated and honoured in accordance with his worth'.[60] In the one case, we have *mathematical* equality, which simply corresponds to the law of numbers; in the other, we have *geometrical* equality, which preserves the idea of

---

54   *The Republic*, Book 8, 558c.

55   *Politics*, Book Three, 1180a, 11 ff.

56   Thucydides, *History of the Peloponnesian War*, Book II, text 37.

57   *Op. cit.*, vol. 1, p. 39.

58   Isocrates (436-338 BCE) was the most influential rhetorician of his day. (Ed.)

59   Isocrates, *Areopagiticus*, 21-22.

60   Isocrates, *Nicocles*, 14.

proportion. According to Aristotle, 'equality is of two kinds, numerical and proportional'.[61] and the former should not stifle the latter. This distinction recurs again and again in philosophical texts. It corresponds to the opposition drawn by Jean Bodin between 'numerical proportion' and 'geometric proportion'.[62] Geometrical equality obeys a classical principle: *suum cuique*, 'to each according to his merits' (*jedem das Seine*, as Frederick I used to say).[63] When turned into a social goal, numeric equality inevitably leads to levelling.

It is quite clear that modern liberal democracies, which are steeped in an egalitarian ideology with its origins in Christianity, have largely promoted a *numeric* conception of equality. According to this conception, the equality of political rights derives from an equality of nature, whose progressive accomplishment is presented as an ideal. This 'natural' equality cannot be empirically proven: it is thus exposed as a 'moral requirement', which is to say, a belief.[64] Geometrical equality, in contrast, rests on reality. Democracies inspired by it do not go against the idea of merit. Political equality, which is based on citizenship, and equality of opportunities, which is aimed not at bringing about equal conditions but at ensuring that social inequalities will not derive from privileges or sheer chance, are both equalities which remain *external* to man. They are but a *means* to bring about a social situation deemed more suitable for the chosen *optimal condition*.

Based on these considerations, it is possible to challenge a number of assumptions, such as that democracy necessarily implies a weak power, which historically replaced 'absolute powers'. Throughout the history of Europe, most monarchies have been far weaker—and less omnipresent—than the modern states, in terms of both resources

---

61 *Politics*, Book 5, Chapter 1, 1301a, 25 ff.

62 Jean Bodin, *Six Books of the Commonwealth* (Oxford: Blackwell, 1955), p. 205.

63 Frederick I (1657-1713) was the first King of Prussia. He gave this motto to the Order of the Black Eagle, which he founded, and which was the highest order of knights in Prussia. The German military police continue to use this motto to this day. (Ed.)

64 It is clear that modern democratic theory has yet to derive any lesson from the recent discoveries made in the life sciences, and particularly from the disproving of the idea that 'natural' equality exists among humans. I would here refer to Julien Cheverny's *Haro sur la démocratie* (Paris: Mame, 1973), which denounces 'politicians' great fear of the Tree of Life' and invites socialists to agree with eugenics (*Des incompatibilités du démocratique et du génétique*, Chapter Three, pp. 119-152; *Eugénisme et socialisme*, Chapter Four, pp. 153-197).

and means. 'Divinely appointed' kings were merely the depositories of a sacred power and used to govern 'with their councils'. (Down to Louis XIV, to give only one example, the Parliament in France had the right to refuse to register fiscal edicts). Tocqueville writes, 'In the centuries of aristocracy that preceded our own, there were very powerful private individuals and a highly debilitated social authority. The very image of society was obscure and was constantly getting lost among all the various powers that ruled over citizens.'[65] It is modern democracies which have limited the power of private citizens, while substantially strengthening 'social authority'. Claude Polin goes so far as to write, 'Prior to the development of the idea of popular sovereignty, men had never even imagined ... that any human power could truly be absolute'.[66] Far from having replaced a powerful authority with a weaker one, modern democracies have, on the contrary, set up popular sovereignty as a (theoretically) *unlimited* power. Under the *Ancien Régime*,[67] the word 'sovereign' simply meant *superior*; besides, this is the etymological meaning of the word.[68] The sovereign prince, constrained by his duties towards the people, was never considered a free man, neither with respect to the goal which he had to pursue, nor with respect to the means he could employ. The underlying characteristic of popular sovereignty, in contrast, is that in principle there is nothing to limit it. It is not the idea of 'absolute power' which democracy rejects, but rather the idea that such power may be the privilege of a single person.

Likewise, democracy does not dispute the validity of the 'law of the strongest'. Every '-cracy' is bound to concentrate 'the greatest force' in a given place, and democracy is no exception to this rule: simply, it claims that popular sovereignty is the force before which one must bow. The majority principle too, in a way, is a law of the strongest. Force is made to rest upon voting, which expresses not so much truth as power. Already Pascal had written, 'Why does one follow the

---

65 *Op. cit.*, p. 828.

66 'De la signification et des conséquences du dogme de la souveraineté populaire', in *La Légitimité*, January-March 1981.

67 This term, translated as 'old regime', refers in this case to the form of government which prevailed in France prior to the French Revolution of 1789. (Ed.)

68 *Op. cit.*

majority? Is it because they have more sense? No, but because they are stronger.'[69]

And what about authority? In 1942, Joseph Schumpeter did not hesitate to define democracy as a *method* enabling the establishment of a strong government charged with authority.[70] Geraint Parry comments, 'Liberty and equality, which were integral parts of the ancient definitions of democracy, are considered by Schumpeter as being essentially foreign to the definition of democracy, however laudable these ideals may be.' Sartori, in turn, writes that, 'Far from despising authority, democracy adopts it as the very formula for its power'.[71] A similar observation is made by Julien Freund concerning *decision-making*. By denouncing 'democraticism', which advocates 'consensus' and 'dialogue' as the only methods of government, Freund emphasises that no society—not even a democratic society—can forgo decision-making. This is implied by the very nature of man as a *decision-making being*: 'Decision-making and choosing are conceptually linked'.[72] Now, decision-making implies the power to translate decisions into practical action.

In Rome, the word 'dictatorship' was used to describe something completely different from what we mean by this term today. Dictators represented not a negation of the Roman form of government, but rather its defenders. Appointed for a given task and a limited period of time, dictators were charged with facing particular needs in difficult moments. Even Rousseau acknowledged the existence of 'emergency situations'. If the Republic is in peril, he argued, a dictatorship of the Roman type, *rei publicae servanda* ('in the service of the republic'), may be justified. In this case, dictatorship is not a threat to popular sovereignty, but rather constitutes the only means to preserve it: the 'salvation of the country' takes precedence over the power of the laws.

Hitler writes in *Mein Kampf*, 'Sooner will the camel pass through a needle's eye than a great man be "discovered" by an election.'[73] (But

---

69 Blaise Pascal, *Pensées: Notes on Religion and Other Subjects* (London: J.M. Dent, 1960), p. 55. (Ed.)

70 Joseph Alois Schumpeter, *Capitalism, Socialism, and Democracy* (New York: Harper, 1950).

71 *Op. cit.*

72 'Que veut dire: prendre une décision?' in *Nouvelle École*, 41, autumn 1984, p. 50.

73 Adolf Hitler, *Mein Kampf* (Boston: Houghton Mifflin Co., 1943), p. 81. (Ed.)

this of course did not prevent Hitler himself from being elected.) This classic anti-democratic argument clashes with the fact that in principle democracy has generally been regarded—despite what even certain 'democrats' claim—not as a system incompatible with the notion of an *elite*, but rather as a particularly safe tool for identifying and promoting an elite. According to Aristotle, elections, insofar as their aim is to seek out the best men, are by their very nature aristocratic.[74] Elections (from the Latin *eligere*, 'to choose') are a form of selection; the very word 'elite' has the same etymology. Originally, democracy expressed a will to replace privilege with merit at a time when the former no longer appeared to be the logical consequence of the latter. The aim was to replace chance factors (especially birth) with skill. *In theory*, therefore, democracy should not be regarded as an anti-elitist system. It is not elites which it is opposed to, but the way in which these are selected. What regime, after all, does not seek *quality* in government? If democracy charmed so many spirits, this is partly because it was seen as the best means for organising elite turnover. All the authors for whom democracy implies greater 'virtue' and quality (Mannheim,[75] De Madariaga,[76] etc.) insist on the idea that elites are crucial for its proper functioning.

In 1835, De Tocqueville declared, 'It is a lesser question for the partisans of democracy to find means of governing the people, than to get the people to choose the men most capable of governing.' According to Lipset, 'The distinctive and most valuable element of democracy in complex societies is the formation of a political elite'.[77] According to Giovanni Sartori, 'Democracy has functioned only when an aristocracy has governed ... Elites possessing a democratic spirit are not a blemish, but rather the most crucial guarantee of the system .... A democracy will affirm and preserve itself as a government *for* the people only if responsible elites of proven democratic loyalty will pur-

---

74 *Politics*, Book 4, 1300b4.

75 Karl Mannheim (1893-1947) was a Hungarian Jewish sociologist whose most important work was *Ideology and Utopia* (London: Routledge, 1936). (Ed.)

76 Salvador de Madariaga (1886-1978) was a Spanish writer and diplomat who became a vocal opponent of Franco's authoritarian regime in exile. His principal work on democracy was *Democracy versus Liberty? The Faith of a Liberal Heretic* (London: Pall Mall Press, 1958). (Ed.)

77 Seymour Martin Lipset, *The First New Nation* (New Brunswick: Transaction Publishers, 2003), p. 208. (Ed.)

sue this as their goal'.[78] When viewed in this light, Sartori continues, democracy may be defined as an elective polyarchy in which power belongs to those who acquire it via the majority of votes after a competition between rival minorities.[79]

The fact nonetheless remains that the majority principle appears to possess an absolute value, a truth connected to the prestigious character of numbers. But actually, is the majority principle really synonymous with democracy? This is far from an established fact. The crucial idea behind democracy is not that it is the majority which decides, but rather that it is the appointment of leaders by those governed which constitutes the true foundation of legitimacy. In other terms, it is the *people* who are sovereign, not *numbers*. The majority rule is merely a *technique*—possibly one amongst others—aimed at discovering the will of the people. Majority and will cannot be identified with one another *in principle*, but only hypothetically or experimentally. It is for this reason that Rousseau attaches such great importance to his theory of the general will. As Georges Burdeau notes, 'As sheer numbers have nothing to do with the juridical and political construction of the notion of the people, pre-revolutionary thought was constantly occupied with envisaging popular will as something other than simply the law of the majority'.[80]

According to the opponents of democracy, it is absurd to think that truth stems from numbers and that the majority is right simply because it is the majority. This criticism, however, which is formally justified, once again misses the mark, for the majority principle is not intended to reveal any 'truth'. Simply, it is a *means for decision-making*.

---

78 *Op. cit.*, p. 79.

79 François Perroux goes one step further when he writes that 'the mass of the popular movement in labour democracy will be a mass that believes in happiness and demands the right to enjoy it. It will be the duty of its elites to make it progressively move beyond the empty trifles of quick and easy happiness. From within the mass, these elites will mobilise elements that will gradually attain a different lifestyle, until one day, perhaps, the whole nation, young and back on its feet, will have the courage to wipe off from the pediments of its monuments the words "well-being and freedom" and replace them with "order and duty".' Shortly after, Perroux adds, 'What we mean by aristocratic is he who knows how to speak against his own self-interest. In this respect, the idea of aristocracy is not opposed to that of the people: for the latter is filled with individuals who are either consciously or unconsciously aristocratic', in *La démocratie* (Paris: Domat-Monichrestien, 1946), p. 25.

80 *Op. cit.*, p. 27.

In politics, decision-making does not mean choosing between what is true and what is false; rather, it means choosing between possible options. The majority neither constitutes nor expresses any mathematical truth, but only suggests what should be regarded as being politically convenient. Bertrand de Jouvenel has aptly shown why the categories 'true' and 'false' can rarely be applied to political problems. On the one hand, the latter often involve points of view which are equally 'legitimate' but mutually incompatible. On the other, the solutions to these problems primarily depend on the goal one is pursuing, and which may vary considerably, as ultimately it tends to rest on values and value choices that are not rationally demonstrable.

The best proof of the fact that the majority principle does not express the truth is the rights assigned to minorities. For if truth were simply expressed by numbers, then the minority would have to disappear—in which case the majority would become a substitute for unanimity. This mistake has been made in all ages, both on the Right and on the Left. Is it not the case that French socialists in 1982 accused their opponents of being at fault legally because they were politically in the minority?

III

POPULAR SOVEREIGNTY
AND PLURALISM

Despite what certain authors (such as Burdeau) would argue, the idea of majority rule nowadays is simply wishful thinking: for it is always a minority that governs. But what form do the relations between the governing minority and the ruled majority take in terms of sovereignty, authority and representation? This is the question. From a theoretical point of view, modern democracy is a system which gives the majority the right to appoint rulers and check their actions through a decision-making process. This decision-making and control is essentially exercised by means of voting. The law, on the other hand, is considered democratic when it is the 'expression of the general will' or—at any rate—when it has been ratified by the entire body of citizens. It thus possesses a general character. Now, from this last point two consequences follow which stand in apparent contradiction to previous observations. The first consequence is that democracy can only really be implemented in a direct form: a citizen who delegates his right to ratify (or reject) a law to a representative—even one he has personally elected—is alienating his own autonomy. In other words, he is making use of his liberty only to renounce it. The other consequence is that a genuine democracy requires approval on the part of not merely the majority but of everyone: for only the rule of unanimity ensures respect for the autonomy of each individual. It is easy to see what obstacles this theory faces. What becomes of popular sovereignty in a representative democracy?

Sorel[1] used to say that 'Rousseau's democracy presupposes a society of artisans having the way of life of the old Swiss'.[2] The fact is that Rousseau has often been accused not only of harbouring a rather ill-considered view of man, but also of having fashioned his imaginary citizens after the austere and disciplined inhabitants of Geneva, whose voluntary associations he had seen working so nicely. Yet there is more to Rousseau than just his defects. His way of envisaging the collectivity strikes us as being far more realistic than Montesquieu's.

By adopting a 'holistic' approach, Rousseau does not hesitate to define the people as a veritable collective organism. Speaking of the social contract, he writes, 'This act of association creates a moral and collective body made up of as many members as the assembly has voices, and which receives from this act its unity, its common *self*, its life and its will.'[3] This idea is reminiscent of the Roman allegory of the limbs and the stomach...[4] Against the 'universalist' optimism of his day, Rousseau has the merit of having posited that each nation is driven by its own particular general will. Finally, he also clearly grasped the contradiction that implicitly exists in the dichotomy between *man* and *citizen*. The social contract, which 'removes man from nature' by turning him into a citizen does not entirely reconcile the two terms. Each citizen finds his limit in those who share his citizenship: for on the other side of the border he reverts to the 'state of nature'. In opposition to Christianity, which 'inspires humanity more than patriotism'

---

1   Georges Sorel (1847-1922) was a French philosopher who began as a Marxist and later developed Revolutionary Syndicalism. He advocated the use of myth and organised violence in revolutionary movements. He was influential upon both the Communist and Fascist movements. His primary works are *Reflections on Violence* and *The Illusions of Progress*. (Ed.)

2   From a meeting of the Société française de philosophie, 27 December 1906.

3   Jean-Jacques Rousseau, *The Social Contract and Other Later Political Writings* (Cambridge: Cambridge University Press, 1997), p. 50.

4   This is a reference to the Roman 'Fable of the Stomach', which describes how at one time the limbs of the human body grew tired of having to constantly serve the needs of the stomach, and stopped working in protest one day. At first, the limbs delighted in the complaints from the stomach, but eventually the stomach became quiet because it was too weak from hunger. Soon, the limbs became too weak to move, and shortly thereafter the entire body died. The fable identifies the body with the state, the stomach with the aristocratic patricians, and the limbs with the common people. The fable is reproduced in H. A. Guerber, *The Story of the Romans* (Chapel Hill: Yesterday's Classics, 2006), pp. 95-98. (Ed.)

and tends to 'shape men more than citizens', Rousseau seeks, in his *Considerations on the Government of Poland*—a text written some ten years after *The Social Contract*—to overcome the above dichotomy, no longer by attempting to reconcile 'patriotism' and 'humanity', but rather by suggesting that citizens should be educated to exclusively worship their country. This suggestion leads Rousseau to envisage the possibility of establishing a national religion inspired by Antiquity.[5]

Locke[6] and Montesquieu have spoken in favour of the separation of powers without dismissing the possibility of delegating popular sovereignty to these powers. This theory of the separation of powers derives from the premises of liberal doctrine. It, too, represents a way for the bourgeoisie to divide sovereignty over which it cannot directly exercise perfect control. Such a theory is rarely applied in practice. Judicial power has never really been separate from the others and has never really constituted a political power. The separation between legislative and executive power has, in most cases, been merely formal. The coalescing of powers into the executive continues to be the general rule. Parliaments, which in liberal democracies are meant to express the general will, have almost everywhere experienced a loss of power, both in terms of rights and in actual practice. We are heading towards princedom.

Rousseau, in contrast, rejects all forms of representation. The people, in his view, are not the signatory of any contract with the sovereign: the relation between the two parties is exclusively based on the law. The prince is merely he who executes the will of the people, for the latter remains the sole repository of legislative power. The prince is not the representative of the general will, but merely its instrument: it is the people which govern through him. Magistrates are elected, but they do not *represent* their electors. The people delegate their power but never forego it. The underlying reasoning here is an extremely logical one: if the people are represented, then it is its representatives who are the power-holders, in which case the people are no longer

---

5   Rousseau, on the other hand, also expresses some extremely elitist sentiments, extolling 'sublime geniuses' (in the preface to his *Narcissus*) and 'great men'. In his eyes, individuals are perfectible, whereas in the case of peoples 'perfectibility' means the completion of their decline.

6   John Locke (1632-1704) was an English philosopher of the Enlightenment who is regarded as the most important theorist of liberalism, as his works were extremely important to the development of modern democracy. (Ed.)

sovereign. According to Rousseau, then, popular sovereignty is indivisible and inalienable. All representation is abdication.[7]

Representative democracy, whereby representatives are legitimated via elections to transform the will of the people into acts of government, constitutes the most common political system in Western countries today. 'Genuine' democracy would thus always appear to be naturally linked to representation. Still, the two notions are far from synonymous. The representative system, which made its first appearance long before modern democracy, was initially regarded as something quite distinct and even contrary to democracy. Hobbes and Locke were its main theorists: both posited that through a social contract, the people delegate their sovereignty to a ruler or rulers.

Hobbes posits complete delegation, which gives the monarch absolute sovereignty. Man, left to himself, is regarded as a nasty creature—the state of nature as a form of anarchy—so the best use he can make of his power is to entrust a sovereign with his own protection. The social contract thus safeguards citizens against the general tyranny of the state of nature. Hobbes is an individualist: the people for him are but a collection of individuals, and there can be no 'merging of wills'. According to Locke, who is a liberal and hence a more optimistic philosopher, individuals are only to delegate their sovereignty in exchange for guarantees concerning individual liberties. Sovereignty in this case is delegated along with distinct powers, which are seen as limiting each other. This is the classical theory of the separation of powers. In both cases, nonetheless, popular sovereignty is non-existent, and we are very far indeed from democracy.

There are two very different ways, then, of conceiving 'representation'. The first, which is close to Rousseau's perspective, is the idea of *representation as commission*: voters never forgo their political will, and representatives are simply 'clerks' charged with representing the *will* of the electorate. The second view, of more specifically liberal inspiration, is the idea of *representation as embodiment*: the political will of those

---

7   According to this view, the people hold the legislative power, while the sovereign is assigned the executive. Rousseau uses the expression 'democratic government' to describe an ideal system in which the people are also the repository of the executive power. But he sees a scenario of this kind as requiring too much 'virtue' to be actually feasible. Hence, he writes, 'If there were a people of Gods, it would govern itself democratically. Such a perfect government is not suited to men'—a claim that has often mistakenly been interpreted as a condemnation of all democracy.

represented is here entirely *transferred* over to their representatives, who are not elected in order that they may simply *express* this will, but are rather legitimated through elections to act according to their own will. In the former case, the person elected is held to do only what his electors want; in the latter, each elector via his vote authorises representatives to act as they wish.

The second form of representation, which is the prevalent one in Western democracies, poses a threat to the very idea of popular sovereignty, according to all the evidence. On the one hand, it almost inevitably leads to the formation of a new oligarchy—that of a political class—so much so that the 'power of the people' largely remains an illusion. On the other, as electors have, by voting, delegated their *entire* political will, the ruling power is authorised to show them that they are being 'fully' represented, and hence to deny them the right to intervene politically in personal, professional, or civic matters. All representative democracies thus run the risk of becoming mere 'representative democracies', i.e., of centring their power on the representatives rather than the people who have elected them. Modern democratic governments, as already noted, are systems ruled by intermediaries—or even *born mediators*.[8] 'The indirect democracy of the modern West', Paul Veyne argues, 'is a way of legitimising the power which professional politicians exercise over a passive population'.[9]

In the French political system, a notion can be found that never occurs in Locke, Montesquieu, or Rousseau. This is the most interesting idea of *national sovereignty*. Article 3 of the Declaration of 1789 reads, 'The principle of all sovereignty resides essentially in the nation. No body or individual may exercise any authority which does not proceed directly from the nation.' This formula once again locates the source of popular will within the collective being of the nation, which

---

8   As Léo Moulin has shown, almost all contemporary electoral methods of voting have their origins in the practices of the Church and its monasteries. As the Church naturally could not count on hereditary succession, it soon resorted to elections. First it followed the principle of unanimity, then the rather bizarre one of *sanior pars*: as St. Benedict explained, the 'wisest' members of the community are to vote for those elected. With qualified majority, 'seniority' (greater wisdom) was later attributed to the majority. The Third Lateran Council introduced the principle of majority based on two-thirds of the voters present for papal elections. The Fourth Lateran Council reverted to a simple majority. The Council of Trent finally adopted the secret ballot.

9   'Les Grecs ont-ils connu la démocratie?', *art. cit.*, p. 22.

is envisaged as more than the mere sum of its individual parts. The nation is here assigned the same characteristics Rousseau assigned to the people. This assimilation reflects the history of France, which is primarily the history of a nation-state. It does not stand in contradiction to the spirit of democracy, particularly considering that the idea of *nation*, in the contemporary sense of the term, only really made its appearance with the Revolution. In the French system, the 'representatives' of the people, then, are not so much individuals elected to express the will of the electorate, as people to whom the body of electors has delegated the power of *willing on behalf of the nation*, i.e., of making decisions in the nation's name. This is not popular sovereignty in the classical sense, but neither is it representative democracy in the liberal sense. Sovereignty here resides with a collective body, the nation, whose *independence* thus constitutes an essential condition for the proper functioning of society. The state itself is sovereign insofar as it embodies the nation. The idea of 'international' or transnational authority is in principle ruled out, except as a possible means of cooperation. The primacy of the national interest, too, here finds justification.[10]

Two specific problems must be examined. The first concerns the possibility of the general will taking on a tyrannical character. The second, which stems from this, concerns the way in which the notions of majority, minority and unanimity are to be understood—in other words, the issue of 'pluralism'.

In the light of historical experience, it appears quite possible for the general will to be exercised in an arbitrary manner. Sorel, in particular, noted that many were sceptical about Rousseau's hypothesis of a 'general will that is always right'. Tocqueville also observed that, 'The national will is one of those phrases that intriguers in all times and despots in all ages have most abundantly abused.'[11] In his day, Aristotle had already observed that the people, too, can become despotic and

---

10 In a work that has become a classic, Friedrich Meinecke describes the national interest in the following terms: 'It tells the statesman what he must do to preserve the health and strength of the state. The State is an organic structure whose full power can only be maintained by allowing it in some way to continue growing', from *Machiavellism: The Doctrine of* Raison d'État *and Its Place in Modern History* (New Haven: Yale University Press, 1957), p. 1.

11 *Op. cit.*, p. 62. (Ed.)

turn into 'kingly power: the whole composing one body'.[12] Megabyzus, in the famous discussion reported by Herodotus, speaks of the risk of 'popular tyranny' as a good argument in favour of oligarchy: 'A mob is ineffective, and there is nothing more stupid or more given to brutality. It is intolerable that people should escape from the brutality of a despot only to fall into the brutal clutches of the unruly masses.'[13] After all, everyone knows that autocratic governments can come about through voting and that dictators are sometimes democratically elected, even by plebiscite.

The law of the majority defines the 'general will' as the opinion of half of those expressing themselves plus one. Clearly, this is not a very satisfactory definition, and we have already stated what we think should be made of this. The will of the people instead appears well-founded when it approaches unanimity. It is particularly compelling when, as Jules Monnerot writes, 'on account of a particular circumstance—and distressful situations tend to produce such circumstances—the men of the people act in mutual harmony, so to speak'.[14] This unanimity, however, is no guarantee in itself. The *temporary* character of majorities is another point to consider. If it is the majority that expresses the popular will, can it really evolve without contradicting itself? There is no obvious answer to this question. Finally, decisions taken by the majority can also be *contradictory*, as is illustrated by the paradox famously conceived by Condorcet[15] and reformulated by the economist Kenneth J. Arrow:[16] three majority votes presenting options taken in pairs, with the first defeating the second, which defeats the third, which in turn defeats the initial option.[17]

---

12 *Politics,* Book Four, Chapter Four. (Ed.)

13 Herodotus, *The Histories,* Book Three, 81. (Ed.)

14 Jules Monnerot, *Sociologie de la Révolution* (Paris: Fayard, 1969), p. 538.

15 Nicolas de Condorcet (1743-1794) was a philosopher and Girondist who died after being imprisoned by the revolutionary authorities. His paradox is formulated in his 1785 book, *Essay on the Application of Analysis to the Probability of Majority Decisions.* Several translations and books about the paradox are available in English. (Ed.)

16 Kenneth Joseph Arrow, *Social Choice and Individual Values* (New York: Wiley, 1951).

17 Suppose we have three alternatives, A, B and C, and three citizens who classify them in a decreasing order of preferences as ABC, BCA and CAB respectively. We find that each time, with two votes against one, A beats B, B beats C and C beats A.

Can the will of a *part* of the people, however numerous, be regarded as the *general* will of the people? Is there not an irreducible antinomy between the unity presupposed by 'will' and the diversity implied by the notion of a 'people'? The basic lesson given here is the obvious fact that political conscience is not homogeneous: even within a uniform system of values, human diversity will express itself through mutually contradictory opinions and preferences.

In 411 BCE, the people's assembly in Athens democratically voted... for the suppression of democracy. The dilemma we are facing becomes evident as soon as we raise the question as to whether this choice was compliant with democracy. The same is true when the majority votes in favour of dictatorship and the 'general will' veers towards tyranny. The same is also the case each time the majority of the people vote in favour of options that many eminent democrats consider unacceptable. After all, Socrates was very democratically sentenced to death. In France today it is quite likely that a popular poll would lead to the re-establishment of the death penalty and the adoption of strict measures to curb immigration—and this is probably the reason why those in power make sure not to consult public opinion on such subjects. The difficulty we are facing here clearly has to do with judgement criteria. What are the criteria for determining that a given majority is voting 'well' in some case and 'badly' in others?

The most common answer is that political decision-making should not go against certain 'moral values'. But this answer is far from satisfactory. On the one hand, how can one defend the idea of popular sovereignty while also arguing, against the general will, in favour of a form of authority that does not coincide with it? Either the people are sovereign, in which case the expressions of their will cannot be condemned; or their will, too, is subject to a greater authority, in which case the people are no longer sovereign. On the other hand, this sort of reasoning simply results in making politics dependent upon morals, which is to say that it denies the former the status of an autonomous category with a distinctive essence and specific means of its own, something many authors deem unacceptable—and not without reason.[18] Finally, it is clear that the value of the 'moral values' usually

---

Arrow has thus shown that this 'perverse mechanism' characterises almost all voting preferences, and as such is a fundamental property of the rule of the majority.

18 We shall refer here to Julien Freund, *L'essence du politique* (Paris: Sirey, 1978).

invoked can itself be called into question, particularly considering that a range of morals exist which are not necessarily mutually compatible, and that the notion of absoluteness is completely meaningless when applied to human affairs[19]—the most reasonable position being to maintain not that politics is 'immoral', but that it has *morals of its own.*

Another answer often given in liberal milieus and intended to prevent 'popular tyranny' is to appeal to the law. This answer is informed by a 'managerial' view of democracy, whereby the institutional and legislative machine is deemed capable of facing all situations. 'The root idea behind this managerial conception is that democracy is a "political system" (as they say) which can be adequately defined in terms of—can be fully reduced to—its mechanical arrangements. Democracy is then seen as a set of rules and procedures, and *nothing but* a set of rules and procedures, whereby majority rule and minority rights are reconciled into a state of equilibrium. If everyone follows these rules and procedures, then a democracy is in working order.'[20] Overestimating the virtuousness of the law poses new problems.[21] A given law may well be far from legitimate. The impersonal power of the law may also prove more tyrannical—and more enduringly so—than the personal power of a despot. Besides, despite what liberals would have us believe, no legislation exists prior to political institutions; rather, it is political will that creates legislation.[22]

The letter and the spirit of democracy are two different things, and the contrast between the two harbours further uncertainties. Can highly 'democratic' goals be reached by resorting to undemocratic means? This political variant of the old debate on the legitimacy of

---

19 It is also worth mentioning that, from an experimental point of view, 'moral policies' have regularly led to tragic mistakes and catastrophic results. In this field more than in any other, it is indeed the case that the road to hell is paved with good intentions.

20 Irving Kristol, *Reflections of a Neoconservative* (New York: Basic Books, 1983), p. 50.

21 Strictly speaking, besides, it is hard to see how 'popular tyranny' may be explained from a liberal standpoint. If societies are simply comprised of rational individuals who always pursue their own 'best interest', and if despotism is regarded as something which goes against this interest, then the hypothesis of a tyranny willed and exercised by all (or the majority) is absurd.

22 'The proof? When an unexpected situation occurs, there is no law or legislation that can help face it. Even if a new "law" or "legislation" will formally solve the situation, it will actually derive from decision-making' (Julien Freund, in *Magazine-Hebdo*, 9 November 1984).

means in relation to ends may also be extended to all debates on the limits of 'legality'. It is clear that throughout history, democrats themselves have tended to act as if one's aim could justify one's means. When it comes to replacing dictatorship with democracy, legal means are bound to be ineffective. Unlike Greek democracy, which was not the product of a revolution but rather of a gradual institutional transformation, all legal systems in France since 1789 have been established by means of violent change or 'illegal' acts. In Portugal, democracy was introduced through a *coup d'état* instigated by the army. This is the general rule. It is only once they have become established that democracies can seek to acquire legitimacy through elections. The latter are then meant to record what is taken to be a pre-existent sentiment, which the new circumstances themselves, however, may have brought about. This form of 'retroactive' consensus is generally not regarded as being antidemocratic. As for the issue of knowing whether a law is democratic because it conforms to democratic procedures, or rather because it corresponds to the 'spirit' of democracy—a query rooted in the Greek distinction between written laws, reflecting the power of the *demos*, and unwritten laws, which are closer to norms (*nomoi*)—it is generally only invoked to criticise juridical positivism and stress that not all forms of legality are legitimate.

Finally, let us note that problems of this sort do not surface only when 'democratic' forces find themselves facing classic examples of dictatorship. For they also emerge, in a more subtle way, each time a democracy has to face a truly popular upheaval. The classic examples here are those of decolonisation and of the demands made by certain minorities. Most national liberation movements whose legitimacy was later recognised initially fought against democratic regimes. This was the case, for instance, with the FLN in Algeria[23] and is still the case today with the IRA in Northern Ireland.[24] An argument which

---

23 The Front de Libération Nationale (National Liberation Front) was founded in 1954 as an underground guerrilla and terrorist group which, among other groups, led the successful fight against French colonial rule in Algeria. After independence was achieved in 1962, the FLN established itself as the only legitimate political party in Algeria, and has ruled continuously up to the present day. (Ed.)

24 The Irish Republican Army has been the name of a series of underground insurgent and terrorist groups in Ireland from 1921 until the present day that seek to gain independence for Northern Ireland from the United Kingdom. De Benoist is referring to Sinn Féin, a political party that began as an offshoot of the IRA in the

the French Socialist government resorted to in October 1984 to justify the extraditon of Basque terrorists who had taken refuge in France, but who were wanted by the Spanish government, was that their actions were illegitimate as they were directed against the authority of a democratic country. This kind of reasoning is truly amazing. The same observation could actually have led to the conclusion that Spanish democracy is not genuinely democratic, for if there is a conflict between popular will and formal democracy, is it not the former that ought to prevail?

In whatever terms we may choose to address this issue, it always seems to lead to the same conclusion: one cannot maintain that the people is the ultimate repository of power while at the same time preventing it from using this power in the way it pleases.

The notion of popular sovereignty, at least in principle, implies the law of unanimity. Now, all evidence suggests that the latter is almost impossible to follow. The question, then, is what the meaning and implications of the notion of majority may be. It is quite clear that this notion can be treated as either a *dogma* or a *technique*. In the former case, the majority is a substitute for unanimity; in the latter, it is merely an expedient.

It is clear why this conception of the majority can prove dangerous. Since the majority speaks the truth—and in absolute terms—then those who have been elected by suffrage will embody the truth. All resistance to their will is thus rendered antidemocratic: 'The leader of such a democracy is irremovable, for the nation, having once spoken, cannot contradict itself. He is, moreover, infallible ... It is reasonable and necessary that the adversaries of the government should be exterminated in the name of popular sovereignty, for the chosen of the people acts within his rights as representative of the collective will, established in his position by a spontaneous decision.'[25] The nations of eastern Europe are democracies of this sort. Marx had

---

1970s. Although it has long been a part of the legitimate government of Northern Ireland, its continuing links to its more militant parent are still well-known, even if not officially acknowledged. (Ed.)

25 Robert Michels, *Political Parties: A Sociological Study of the Oligarchical Tendencies of Modern Democracy* (New York: Hearst's International Library Co., 1915), p. 218. Michels (1976-1936) was a German sociologist and student of Max Weber whose ideas were influential upon the Fascists. He came to embrace Fascism himself. (Ed.)

already interpreted divergences in opinion as resulting from class differences. Hence, the establishment of a classless society must naturally coincide with the establishment of unanimity. For Lenin, just as for Robespierre, the minority has no rights.

Of course, it has been noted that a tyranny of the majority is still preferable to a tyranny exercised by a minority, for the former will necessarily oppress fewer people. But at best this is only true in the case of all things being equal. Considering how the notion of power changes and how power is distributed, reasoning of this kind becomes meaningless in the face of modern totalitarianism, which may be defined not as the tyranny exercised by a few over many, but as the despotism of all over each.

Some authors nonetheless argue that unanimity is a goal less remote that one might imagine. For the minority not to forgo its opinions but rather to accept that only those of the majority will prevail may be considered a form of unanimity. 'The majority', René Capitant writes, 'is thus promoted—with unanimous consensus—to the rank of arbiter of the general will.'[26]

The perspective changes completely if the majority principle is instead regarded as a mere technique. According to the liberal school, in particular, all forms of domination are anti-democratic, including those exercised over the minority. Therefore not only democracy cannot be reduced to the mere rule of the majority, but it is the rights assigned to the minority (or the opposition) that become an essential criterion to assess the proper functioning of democracy. These rights limit the power of the majority, even if this issues from the 'sovereign people'. The underlying belief behind this conception of democracy is best expressed by Francesco Nitti: 'The majority is not the entire nation, nor does it always represent its best part. It is often minorities that develop the most lofty ideas and feelings.'[27] The reasoning here is the following: if the opposition has no rights, then the majority becomes permanent. Now, if the majority cannot become the minority, then we no longer have democracy, as the rule of the democratic game is precisely that majorities can change. According to this view, the majority is an expedient: as unanimity is impossible to achieve on account of the divergence of opinions, power is assigned to the

---

26 *Démocratie et participation politique*, p. 11.

27 *La démocratie*, vol. 2, p. 136.

majority, which nonetheless only possesses relative value and limited authority as it is destined to change. 'The majority, in terms of both public opinion and those elected', Claude Leclercq wrote, 'makes no claim to represent the will of the country; overall it may be more likely to express it than the minority, but it may also be mistaken. In any case, it cannot claim to be alone in expressing this will. Hence, it must acknowledge the minority as a value in itself'.[28] Likewise, political rights are given to the opposition, which Guglielmo Ferrero describes in much the same spirit as 'an organ of popular sovereignty as essential as government'.[29] By extension, social minorities will also be granted political rights. Democracy thus becomes *pluralistic*.

There is much truth in the above argument. The majority principle is indeed but a technique and democracy cannot be reduced to it. It is not the majority which determines what is 'true' and what is 'false'; and when taken as a dogma, it can lead to tyranny. Still, this 'liberal' approach is not quite satisfactory. There is a great risk that as it gradually extends, 'pluralism' may dissolve the notion of *people*, which is the very basis of democracy.

The very fact of arguing that the general will possesses only a relative value cannot easily be reconciled with idea of popular sovereignty: by definition, sovereignty cannot be divided. The way in which the political rights assigned as a guarantee to the opposition are commonly assimilated to the rights from which social minorities wish to benefit is itself problematic: for political categories cannot always be transposed on a social level. This may lead to a serious failure to distinguish between *citizen minorities* and *non-citizen groups* installed—whether temporarily or not—in the same land as the former. 'Pluralism' may here be used as a rather specious argument to justify the establishment of a 'multicultural' society that severely threatens national and folk identity, while stripping the notion of the people of its essential meaning.

But 'pluralism' also faces a number of other difficulties. First of all, it is a matter of knowing in what domains it must (and can) be exercised. On the level of political action, for instance, it is clear that a government that in the name of 'fairness' seeks to represent all the points of view that are expressed or exist would soon become impotent. Each

---

28   Claude Leclercq, *Le principe de la majorité* (Paris: Colin, 1971), p. 70.

29   Guglielmo Ferrero, *The Principles of Power* (New York: G.P. Putnam's Sons, 1942).

government only represents a majority, be it one that stems from elections or from party agreements.

As far as voting is concerned, election by majority vote appears to be ill-suited to the requirements of pluralism. In this system, voters whose candidates have been defeated are *not* represented—even if in theory those elected should represent all the voters in their constituencies, including the people who did not vote for them.[30] All seats are assigned to the majority, while the minority has none. This process leads to the mutual integration of political parties, in the sense that the number of parties will tend to decrease, as by merging with others each will increase its chances of becoming elected.

Proportional representation, in contrast, is perfectly adequate from a pluralistic standpoint. The only inconvenience is that it is far less democratic. This system bears two direct consequences that go against the principle of popular sovereignty. The first is that, in this form of representation, majorities are no longer formed directly through voting, but rather through the games played by the parties for which one has voted. As they no longer lead to the establishment of a majority (but rather of a *plurality* of possible majorities), elections no longer express the will of the country. The second consequence is that governments will necessarily consist of coalitions. Parties here no longer have to respond directly to voters, since their actions chiefly depend on parliamentary and governmental arrangements. No party can thus offer its voters assurance of the fact that it will implement its platform: even if it comes into power it will have to strike a compromise with the platforms of other parties in the coalition. Under these conditions, citizens are bound to feel that their choices are ineffective, and this in turn fosters abstentionism and contributes to political apathy. Besides, as this system encourages the multiplying of parties, its political life will be marked by instability, impotence and irresponsibility. 'Proportional representation breaks the will of the people'.[31]

---

30 This is a classical paradox. The person elected must act as a partisan up until the elections, but must then prove capable—after the elections—of transcending his own personal inclinations. A head of state elected through universal suffrage will behave like a party leader at first, but will then attempt to present himself as the 'president of all citizens'. These two requirements cannot easily be reconciled (even when there is a genuine will to do so).

31 Michel Debré, in *Magazine-Hebdo*, 19 October 1984.

Another classic problem concerns the plurality of opinions. Modern democracies, in theory, guarantee freedom of opinion, as they do freedom of expression. The authorities, in other words, have no right to prevent citizens from thinking whatever they like and from using whatever means are available to express their own opinions and find an audience for themselves. Yet, this immediately raises the problem presented by those opinions which are opposed not merely to the orientations of the ruling government or system, but the form of government and system in themselves. This is the case with anti-democratic or 'revolutionary' opinions, whether they are of the Left or of the Right. We are thus faced with a dilemma. If the authorities really assign the same rights to all, then they are indirectly legitimising the action of those wishing to destroy the system they represent—hence, their behaviour is suicidal. If, in contrast, they exclude a certain number of tendencies or opinions from the pluralistic game, then they are going against their own principles, and the crude question emerges as to the *criteria* adopted for exclusion and of the competence and good faith of those responsible for it.

Furthermore, one may wonder to what extent rights and duties can be treated separately. Does the right to freedom of expression include the right to *radical* opposition? If so, are not the authorities acknowledging that they are transgressing the mandate conferred upon them (and which one may imagine includes safeguarding the stability of the ruling system)? But if the former right excludes the latter, is there not a great risk of freedom of expression only benefiting those from whom the ruling system has nothing to fear, severely limiting the political choices open to the 'sovereign people'? Besides, in the name of what may it be argued that the present system is so excellent that we have the *duty* not to try and change it?

In the Federal Republic of Germany,[32] Right-wing and Left-wing 'extremists' are barred by law from certain professions—particularly public offices. The pretext for these 'professional bans' (*Berufsverbote*) is the fact that they target individuals whose actions go against the fundamental legal provisions serving as a constitution for the FRG. But this is a questionable argument—and indeed it is strongly questioned.

---

32 At the time Mr. de Benoist was writing (1985), Germany was still divided into East (Communist) and West (liberal-democratic) Germany. The Federal Republic was the government of West Germany. However, the *Berufsverbote* remains in effect in present-day Germany. (Ed.)

On the one hand, a large number of 'radicals' affected by these measures claim they respect the Constitution. On the other—and most importantly—it is hard to see why opinions should be considered legitimate only when they meet the requirements of a contractual document as vague and temporary as a constitution. Limiting pluralism to the 'constitutional structure' of a country: is this not slipping into the dullest juridical positivism? If the people are sovereign and minorities possess only relative value, it is rightly impossible to limit the people's choices. To this a moral argument may be added: there is little merit in granting freedom of expression to those whose opinions hardly differ from one's own. A similar attitude soon becomes an excuse to grant freedoms only to people of whom we are sure beforehand will not make 'ill' use of them. It means believing that the ruling system is so excellent that once it has been established, we have the right to proscribe all possibilities of choosing a different one. All radical dissent—which is to say, all genuine dissent—is thus banned. But can we still call this a democracy?

Saint-Just famously declared, 'No freedom for the enemies of freedom.' The only inconvenience is that for Saint-Just, freedom was not incompatible with the Reign of Terror. Still, this does not prevent propagandists nowadays from invoking his formula. Many 'liberals' acknowledge each person's right to express his opinions... provided these do not challenge the ideological assumptions to which they are accustomed. A few years ago, a leader of the LICRA[33] stated, 'It is no threat to freedom of expression to bring an end to the actions of an organisation that dares present itself as anti-democratic.' This is tantamount to saying that in democracy, only democrats enjoy freedom of expression. Along the same lines, one could say that in a Fascist regime there is perfect freedom to express Fascist opinions, and that in a Communist regime all opinions are welcome, provided they are Marxist. How freedom may benefit from all this is far from clear.

Another 'solution' consists of denying certain opinions the status of opinions, for instance by making them fall under the blows of the law, turning them into crimes. In France, for instance, racism and anti-Semitism are brought to court because they allegedly stir 'racial

---

33 The Ligue Internationale Contre le Racisme et l'Antisémitisme (International League Against Racism and Anti-Semitism) was established in 1926 and continues to exist today, maintaining chapters in several countries. (Ed.)

hatred'. Socialism and Marxism, in contrast, are not struck by the law, despite the fact that according to the same reasoning they objectively stir 'social hatred'. (Structurally, the theory of class struggle can hardly be distinguished from that of the struggle among races.) Besides, if we establish the principle that any systematic criticism coincides with an indirect instigation to commit illegal acts against the people or groups criticised, politics would soon be reduced to silence. It is also clear that there are some people who enjoy a sort of statutory immunity guaranteed by law in our society and others who do not. The right to criticism would appear to be a necessary corollary of the freedom of expression.[34] Once more, therefore, we are caught in a deadlock.

The risk posed by unchecked pluralism is equally evident. Noting how most forms of government are undermined by social divisions, already Plato feared that democracy would encourage licentiousness and lead to anarchy. His *Republic* is an attempt to overcome these dangers. Despite what is frequently argued—for we should not be fooled by the liberal comparison between the Platonic city and modern Communism—Plato's model does not invoke people's rights to possess similar goods as much as the need to establish an organic agreement amongst all. Plato wishes to foster harmony and prevent the clash of social classes and parties. If he slips into egalitarianism, it is only in pursuit of this goal. Plato believes that harmony will result from homogenisation, forgetting that cities do not consist of men similar to one another. Aristotle later showed that genuine solidarity stems from the mutual complementing of intrinsically different parts—not from the erosion of differences.

The harmony Plato dreamed of nonetheless remains a commendable goal. Pluralism is a positive notion, but it cannot be applied to everything. We should not confuse the pluralism of values, which is a sign of the break-up of society (since, while values only have meaning in respect to other values, they cannot all have equal footing), with

---

34 An attitude bordering on criminalisation is the argument—resting on emotional and moral grounds—that in certain cases one 'does not have the right to be objective'. Bias thus becomes a duty, so as not to 'trivialise' things and make oneself an accomplice. Along these lines, Claude Sarraute writes: 'When it is a matter of crimes against humanity, the notions of absolute, total good and evil cannot be ignored' (*Le Monde*, 3-4 December 1979). This is a disconcerting remark: it is asking judges to take a biased stand in order to satisfy metaphysical requirements. We know only too well what exhortations of this sort can lead to.

the pluralism of opinions, which is a natural consequence of human diversity. The pluralism of sources of inspiration, moreover, does not coincide with that of powers: 'In a society whose political life is legally organised, there cannot be room for multiple centres of sovereign power'.[35] Freedom of expression is thus destined to end not where it interferes with others' freedom (this being a liberal formula which could easily be shown to be hardly meaningful), but rather where it stands in contrast to the general interest, which is to say to the possibility for a folk community to carve a destiny for itself in line with its own founding values.

---

35 Georges Burdeau, *La démocratie*, p. 118.

IV

THE CRISIS OF DEMOCRACY

It is difficult to tell whether such a thing as democracy ever really existed. In order to determine to what extent democratic practice differs from the ideal or theory of democracy, we should first of all agree on what criteria to adopt. This in turn raises a whole series of problems. Besides, are vagaries not the rule in all human affairs? Is there not a necessary gap between projects and their implementation? While these questions may be perfectly legitimate ones, the fact remains that public opinion nowadays appears to have been hit by a huge wave of disappointment. Democracy is disappointing.[1] Why?

The theme of the betrayal of the democratic ideal by democratic practice has long been a recurrent one among both the partisans of democracy (who hope to correct its defects) and its enemies (who wish to expose its hypocrisy or prove its infeasibility). Marxists criticise the 'formal democracy' of the liberals and aim to replace it with economic and social democracy, which in line with the requirements of their cause they regard as the 'real democracy'.[2] Yet, pejorative use of the expression 'formal democracy' has also been made by the revolutionary syndicalist Georges Sorel and the neoconservative thinker Arthur Moeller van den Bruck[3] (*formale Demokratie*).

---

1   See, for instance, Claude Julien, *The Suicide of the Democracies* (London: Calder & Boyars, 1975); and Julien Cheverny, *Haro sur la démocratie*.

2   Marxism is playing with words when it takes the term 'formal' to mean 'deceiving', since 'formal' is not the opposite of 'real'.

3   Arthur Moeller van den Bruck (1876-1925) was one of the principal authors of the German metapolitical Conservative Revolutionary movement. His principal work

According to Sorel, 'formal democracy' —what today we would call liberal democracy—simply serves to reinforce the rule of the bourgeoisie. In *The Illusions of Progress* (1908), Sorel criticises the 'dogmas of popular sovereignty, of the righteousness of the general will, of parliamentary representation'; he depicts deputies as 'secular bishops to whom popular acclamation has given an indefinite power', and finally denounces bourgeois democracy as a form of 'decadence' governed by 'destructive instincts' —a characterisation later adopted by Maurras.[4] 'In our modern democracies', Sorel writes, 'almost everyone feels free from the past, is without a deep love of the home, and thinks but little of future generations; deluded by the mirage of speculative riches which would come from the cleverness of their minds rather than from a serious participation in material production, they think only of royally enjoying windfalls. Their true bailiwick is the big city where men pass like shadows; political committees have taken the place of the old "social authorities" destroyed by revolutions, whose descendants have abandoned a country forgetful of its past, and who have been replaced by people living in the new fashion.'[5]

Aristotle used to say that ultimately only two forms of government exist: oligarchy and democracy—all others being mere variations or deviations of these. Montesquieu is expressing mostly the same idea when he writes, 'In a republic when the people as a body have sovereign power, it is a democracy. When the sovereign power is in the hands of a part of the people, it is called an aristocracy.'[6] Posed in such terms, the above alternative can only lead to disenchantment for democrats: for as Robert A. Dahl[7] and Giovanni Sartori[8] have shown, all modern Western democracies are nothing but elective *polyarchies*.

---

is *Germany's Third Empire* (London: George Allen & Unwin, 1934), in which he discusses formal democracy. (Ed.)

4   Georges Sorel, *From Georges Sorel, Volume 2: Hermeneutics and the Sciences* (New Brunswick: Transaction Publishers, 1990), pp. 85-86. (Ed.)

5   Georges Sorel, *From Georges Sorel: Essays in Socialism and Philosophy* (Oxford: Oxford University Press, 1987), p. 254. (Ed.)

6   Montesquieu, *The Spirit of the Laws* (Cambridge: Cambridge University Press, 1989), p. 10. (Ed.)

7   Robert A. Dahl, *A Preface to Democratic Theory* (Chicago: University of Chicago Press, 1956).

8   *Op. cit.*

The representative system exudes its own logic. In a representative democracy, the people delegates elected politicians with the duty of implementing its 'decisions'. Little, however, is carried out by those elected in person: for they in turn delegate various tasks and missions to their advisers, officials and 'experts'—individuals whose work hardly depends on people's votes. Besides, political power is but one form of power among others. Power in society is also exercised by economic bodies, cultural institutions, financial groups, media, etc., where the people in charge, who wield genuine power in terms of *influence* and *decision-making*, are also never elected. Likewise, considerable power is held by officials, who exercise an even more direct influence upon society: the proportion of government officials in the French political class has steadily increased (from 31 per cent in the National Assembly of 1973 to 53.15 per cent in 1981). Overall, then, elections only concern a very small number of those wielding some form of power. In liberal democracies, the power of people *nominated* or *co-opted* far exceeds that of the people *elected*.

Even parties, which play such a crucial role in politics, operate in a rather undemocratic fashion. Based on an in-depth study of political parties, already in 1910 Robert Michels formulated his 'iron law of oligarchy'.[9] Michels observed that parties are primarily organisations, and that every organisation is necessarily hierarchical; under the influence of a professional political class, parties unavoidably tend to take an oligarchic form. 'Democracy leads to oligarchy, and necessarily contains an oligarchical nucleus', Robert Michels wrote—an observation he found most depressing. A classic counter-argument advanced by Sartori is that, in a democratic society, democracy is expressed not by structures but by interactions: what matters is not whether parties are oligarchic, but whether the competition among them is truly 'free'. It is easy to see how this typically liberal counter-argument turns the theory of democracy into an adjunct of the *theory of competition*, in contrast to classical doctrine, which makes it an adjunct of the *theory of the mandate*.

Opposed to one another, parties all agree that the party system must be preserved—just as politicians all agree that political institutions must be preserved. Most importantly, parties are ends in themselves: the organisation's *raison d'être* becomes the organisation itself.

---

9   Michels, *op. cit.*

Parties all claim to be defending the common interest, when actually they are all defending their own power and are chiefly concerned with extending their own electoral strongholds. The competition opposing them, then, brings managerial minorities into play that face one another through various strategies and combinations largely unaffected by public opinion. 'In the United States', Claude Julien writes, 'the national conventions that select presidential candidates are a kind of circus designed to camouflage the power struggles and the often scandalous behind-the-scenes negotiations and deals that nevertheless sooner or later come to light.'[10] On the other hand, candidates for the most part get elected not because of their personal qualities, but for the labels they bear and the prestige of the parties presenting them. Now, party leaders themselves are not always elected, while a politician who is must conform to the line adopted by the movement or organisation to which he belongs. Hence, the mediation that representatives are meant to exercise between assemblies and their own constituencies becomes rather meaningless. No party is forced to take account of the point of view of its elected candidates, as it is responsible for their electoral success in the first place and knows full well that it would be enough to revoke their investiture for them not to be re-elected. In Britain no politician can be elected unless he has been adopted and presented as a party candidate (Churchill had first-hand experience of this in his day).[11] Moreover, an MP who is a member of the majority cannot vote against his own government. Parliamentary debates, then, are a mere ritual. The holding of several mandates, a phenomenon which is becoming increasingly widespread,[12] further worsens the situation, since it prevents elite turnover, concentrates the political class, leads to an overlap between the national and local level—to the

---

10 *The Suicide of the Democracies*, p. 129. (Ed.)

11 Churchill's first political office was as a Conservative member of Parliament from Oldham, to which he was elected in 1900. He soon began opposing many of the Conservatives' goals, however, and was deselected by his constituency through a vote of no confidence in 1903. This led to Churchill crossing the floor to join the Liberals, which helped him to retain office. He remained there until he lost his seat in 1922. He attempted to run as an independent in 1923 but was defeated, causing him to rejoin the Conservatives in 1924 and again win office. (Ed.)

12 In 1968, 67 per cent of French MPs held two or more successive mandates. This percentage has gradually increased, reaching 82.1 per cent in December 1982.

point of confusing the two—and finally favours the oligarchical control of parties over men and electoral strongholds.

Democracy has changed. It was initially intended to serve as a
means for the people to participate in public life by appointing representatives. It has instead become a means for these representatives to
acquire popular legitimacy for the power which they alone hold. The
people are not governing through representatives: it is electing representatives who govern by themselves. Who is representing what? The
very notion of 'representation' is in crisis.[13]

'Universal suffrage is the equivalent for political power for the
working class', Marx wrote on 25 August 1852.[14] But we know what
happened instead: the working class has not come into power at
all—and certainly not through elections. Rousseau proved more of a
realist concerning the English system of which Montesquieu was so
fond. He observed, 'The English people thinks it is free; it is greatly
mistaken, it is free only during the election of Members of Parliament;
as soon as they are elected, it is enslaved, it is nothing. The use it makes
of its freedom during the brief moments it has it fully warrants its los-
ing it.'[15] Many other authors have made similar observations. In a representative system, 'citizens emerge from dependence for a moment
to indicate their master and then return to it' (Tocqueville).[16] It is not
so much the people that elects, as candidates who are elected. Voters
are in theory called to *decide*, but actually they are merely *consulted*.
In principle, candidates wish to be elected in order to implement their
own ideas. In practice, all they care about is getting elected—hence
candidates often prefer to win the elections by following other peoples'
ideas rather than to follow their own and lose. 'According to democratic standards', Serge-Christophe Kolm writes, 'this is nothing but
a hijacking of power—a vast plundering of popular sovereignty at the
hands of a clique …. Elections are a ceremony for bestowing legitimacy: the people crown a candidate or consecrate a president without

---

13 In August 1984, *Le Monde* published a series of articles devoted to the 'crisis of the
    representative system'.

14 From a letter Marx published in the *New York Tribune* on that date, included in
    Karl Marx, *Selected Writings* (Oxford: Oxford University Press, 1977), p. 332. (Ed.)

15 Rousseau, *op. cit.*, p. 114. (Ed.)

16 Tocqueville, *op. cit.*, p. 819. (Ed.)

having much choice in the matter. Ballots resemble psycho-social forms of diversion or votive feasts more than sovereign elections.'[17]

The fact that the electoral body is so large further strengthens people's impression that voting is 'useless'. 'When we ask where liberty is', Bertrand de Jouvenel writes, "they" refer us to the ballots in our hands; over the vast machine which keeps us in subjection we have this one right: we, the ten- or twenty- or thirty-millionth of the sovereign, lost in the vast crowd of our fellows, can on occasion take a hand at setting the machine in motion.'[18] Clearly, there appears to be only a slight difference between not voting and exercising a thirty-millionth of the power to decide. When elections concern a very high number of voters, the likelihood of single votes proving decisive—of an individual having the role of 'pivotal vote', as the Americans say—is minimal, particularly when candidates' platforms tend to converge. Alienation *through massification* acts as a powerful demoralising factor. Even those who do vote are aware that there are few statistical chances of their votes actually influencing the final outcome.

The question arises, then, as to why people continue to vote. Serge-Christophe Kolm[19] has shown that the motivations given for voting are essentially irrational, if not absurd. The most common reason invoked is that 'if everyone were to abstain', decisions would be made without one influencing them in the slightest. So people choose to participate in elections in which each vote, considered individually, has *no* influence upon the final outcome...

But there are also other reasons why voting has largely fallen into disrepute. One of these is candidates' lack of reliability. Few candidates keep their promises once they have been elected. (Once they have come into power, many actually adopt policies which are exactly the opposite of those they had originally announced.) After all, why should they keep their promises? They are hardly obliged to do so. To justify themselves, politicians can always invoke changes of circumstances and external pressure. In theory, of course, they run the risk of not getting re-elected (assuming they intend to stand as candidates again); but this is only a minor risk. Few voters remember the promises

---

17 Serge-Christophe Kolm, *Les élections sont-elles la démocratie?* (Paris: Éditions du Cerf, 1977), pp. 12-13.

18 Bertrand de Jouvenel, *On Power*, pp. 316-317. (Ed.)

19 *Op. cit.*

made by a politician in previous elections. If need be, well-orchestrated propaganda will make them forget. What most voters chiefly take into account is the *recent* behaviour of candidates; hence, once elected, politicians hasten to take measures they know will prove unpopular or which go against the promises they had previously made, while demagogic measures increase when new elections are approaching.

In order to compensate for this inconvenience, suggestions have been made to shorten politicians' mandates. But this would mean condemning political life to permanent elections, which would further discourage politicians from pursuing long-term plans. Besides, one should not forget that many *necessary* measures are also highly *unpopular*... A better solution might be to adopt a procedure whereby a certain number of citizens can bring new elections about—provided this number is large enough. To some extent, a method of this kind would restore the conditions of the mandate for rule by allowing the people to revoke it at any time. Yet, as one would expect, political parties are not at all willing to accept this kind of reform.

The idea of 'useful voting', which leads people to vote not for the candidate they prefer but rather *against* those they detest the most, also contributes to distort the mechanism. Voting of this sort takes place each time a voter who prefers candidate A votes for candidate B for the simple reason that he regards the latter as being more likely to prevent a candidate C from getting elected. At election time candidates themselves do not hesitate to encourage this form of voting, which clearly reflects citizens' real preferences only in a very approximate way.

It has often been noted that majority rule does not take account of the *intensity* of people's preferences. Lukewarm voters carry as much weight as resolute voters or committed militants: 'Those who are caught between two alternatives and those who strongly prefer one over the other carry the same weight in the choice between them' (S.-C. Kolm).[20] This is only partially made up for by the fact that—all things being equal—abstentionism is generally more common among individuals with less marked preferences.

Neo-liberals have shown particular interest in the possibility of reforming the electoral system in such a way as to take into account the intensity of individual preferences. Theorists from the Virginia

---

20 *Op. cit.*

School[21] (N. Tideman, G. Tullock, etc.), whose views find expression in the journal *Public Choice*, have more specifically sought to develop a 'Demand Revealing Process' (DRP) inspired by the theory of 'voluntary exchange'. The latter is regarded as describing the best possible conditions for the exchange of resources in an economy where everyone consumes an equal share of public goods. The principle behind this mechanism is the attempt to determine the 'price' each voter would be willing to pay for his choice. But surely, one may object, how much individuals are willing to pay depends not only on the intensity of their preferences but also on the economic resources at their disposal! This theory for the evaluation of 'social choices' thus proves extremely complicated and faces a number of impossibilities. Its implementation would probably cause a rise in abstentionsim and would lead to the formation of coalitions striving to reduce the cost of the information required from each individual.

In more general terms, the various researches into 'voting models' that are being increasingly developed in recent years (and the attempts to empirically test them) all suffer from certain defects stemming from their underlying liberal assumptions. Data concerning electoral politics are systematically examined in these studies on the basis of economic models. Voters are treated as 'rational individuals' choosing those options most suited to the pursuit of their own 'best interest'. Now, applying an economic paradigm to politics is problematic not only because it is an operation based on a questionable 'anthropological' approach, but also because the kind of interactions engendered by elections are simply not the same as those produced by the market. An electoral decision certainly results from the summarising of individual votes, yet it remains a *collective* decision; as such, it applies to all, including those people who have expressed an opposite opinion. Consequently, we cannot speak here in terms of 'mutual advantage', as we would in the case of an economic exchange or transaction. All studies in this field have proven disappointing: it is difficult to apply them to reality both because of their abstract character and because it

---

21 The Virginia School of Political Economy refers to a school that is centred around several universities in Virginia that is seen as being closely allied to the Austrian School. (Ed.)

is impossible to take into account all of the factors that contribute to turn individual preferences into collective choices.[22]

Another classic problem is that of the tyranny of money. Aristotle, who regarded democracy as the 'government of the poor' — 'Wherever men rule by reason of their wealth, whether they be few or many, that is an oligarchy'[23] — would be surprised to learn what an important role in the development of modern democracy was played by the kind of financial powers Emmanuel Beau de Loménie[24] has studied in his works on 'bourgeois dynasties'.[25]

It is common knowledge that in liberal democracies money is one of the basic credentials required of all electoral candidates, whether they personally dispose of it or — as is most frequently the case — they manage to raise it for their own profit. With no means of financial support, candidates practically have no chance of getting elected; indeed, they have few chances of even standing as candidates in the first place. To access power one needs money — and power in turn is useful to acquire more money. Obviously, as electoral campaigns are becoming increasingly expensive, financial support is not given for free (unless exceptionally); rather, it is granted in exchange for things voters know nothing about, and which may or may not take the form of specific commitments on a candidate's part. The economic powers with the greatest means at their disposal are clearly also the ones that can exercise the greatest influence on political affairs. This influence is only

---

22 On this matter, see Giovanni Sartori, 'Will Democracy Kill Democracy? Decision-Making by Majorities and by Committees', in *Government and Opposition*, spring 1975; and Thomas Romer and Howard Rosenthal, 'Voting Models and Empirical Evidence', in *American Scientist*, September/October 1984, pp. 465-473. For a critical overview of the DRP, see Jean-Dominique Lafay, 'Intensité des préférences individuelles et choix collectifs. À la recherche des meilleurs systèmes de vote', in *Bulletin SEDEIS*, March 1984, pp. 44-45.

23 *Politics*, Book Three, Chapter Eight, 1279b34-1280a4. (Ed.)

24 Emmanuel Beau de Loménie (1896-1974) was a veteran of the First World War and was briefly involved with Charles Maurras' Action Française in 1919. He soon broke with Mauras before settling into a career as a writer. His work is untranslated. (Ed.)

25 Aristotle's criticism of the power of money should be envisaged in the context of the Ancients' disparagement of commercial activities and mercantile values. 'No trading for the sake of gain', Plato wrote (*Laws*, 847d). For the Greeks, to be rich was to think one could do whatever one pleased (cf. the double meaning of the Latin word *luxuria*).

limited by the means at the disposal of other competing powers. The democratic game is rigged. In 1968, Richard Nixon's victory in the U.S. elections cost the Republican Party 29 million dollars, and Ronald Reagan's in 1984 cost over 40 million (about 25 million of which was spent on television and radio advertising). Serge-Christophe Kolm sums up the situation with the following bitter formula: 'The surest way of getting elected with the majority of votes is to start by gaining the majority of Francs.'[26]

Certainly, to some extent—at least on a small scale—financial support can be replaced by *militancy*: candidates who lack funds can at least attempt to awaken devotion to a cause. Still, experience shows that the parties that stir the most militant devotees are usually the most extremist. 'Moderates' by definition have only a moderate enthusiasm. 'The more extreme opinions get', S.-C. Kolm notes, 'the more are people generally willing to sacrifice and pay to defend them ... Very often, militants and funders are more extremist than ordinary voters'.[27] What should we make, then, of a system in which selfless donations are most common among extremist factions?

The tyranny of money clearly goes hand-in-hand with corruption and financial scandals. People seem to derive some comfort from the idea that scandals are now and then brought to light, which would prove that in democracies information circulates 'freely'. It is curious indeed how democracy manages to pride itself on its own defects. It may be objected that the scandals which do come to light are far fewer than those which do not. One is also led to wonder whether it may not be the system itself that, by its very *nature*, favours such scandals. Montesquieu argued that the risk of corruption is far greater in democracies than in monarchies because in the former regimes power is more diffused, and hence the number of corrupt politicians is bound to be higher.[28]

An author who can hardly be accused of being a Marxist, François Perroux, notes, 'Far from obstructing the affairs of the landed classes, Nineteenth century democracy favoured them. In a formal democracy, it is money that carries power. ... Democracy in the Twentieth century

26 *Op. cit.*, p. 123.

27 *Op. cit.*, p. 119.

28 *Considerations on the Causes of the Greatness of the Romans and Their Decline*, Chapter Three.

will be nothing but an empty word, insofar as it will be confined to the capitalist economy and bourgeois forms of parliamentary liberalism'.[29]

Another problem lies in the fact that in all ages, democracy has stood for the government of public opinion. Elections serve to measure 'public opinion' and polls to get a clearer picture of it. But how are opinions formed? The fact that elections may be free is meaningless if opinion-forming is not. Besides, the very notion of public opinion is open to challenge. Only a small number of people hold opinions that may be regarded as genuine convictions. The vast majority of people have no real opinions but only impressions: vague, contradictory and ill-defined ideas that depend on their moods and infatuations and which are in constant flux, for they are shaped by events, propaganda, and various forms of conditioning. 'Opinions are the most changeable, if not the slackest, of all the choices of the mind', François Perroux again writes. Most importantly, people do not form their opinions independently.

One of the key notions in democratic procedure is precisely information. People's decisions and choices are largely determined by the information they receive. On the other hand, the only way to make oneself known in a democracy is through the media. A candidate nobody talks about stands no chance of getting elected. An event which is not covered by the media is a non-event: it is as if it had never taken place. Now, information is not objective data. Either it is controlled and biased, or it conveys a considerable number of messages that have a mutually *neutralising* effect. In any case, voters are *never* in a position to determine their own opinions. On the one hand, the media wield considerable power, as they shape opinions that are then expressed through voting—and those who *decide* about what information is provided are never elected. On the other hand, through a whole range of methods close to marketing and advertising techniques, it is possible to manipulate public opinion today in ways unknown to the classic propaganda of the past. Popular will is thus being increasingly fabricated by using methods to condition public opinion.

Not only did the spread of democratic procedures fail to prevent the development of conditioning techniques, but the two phenomena went hand-in-hand. The standardisation of 'opinions' and behaviours through the language of advertising—which continues to be based

---

29 *La démocratie*, p. 22. (Ed.)

on stereotypes, while also operating outside the world of advertisement—has now reached striking proportions. Advertising and marketing have taken the place of propaganda. No despotic regime so far had managed to get people to so passively accept a similar *Gleichschaltung*.[30]

Tocqueville, who held the 'tyranny of opinion' to be a form of despotism typical of democracies, argued that it was especially to be found in America. 'What I find most repugnant in America is not the extreme liberty that prevails there but the virtual absence of any guarantee against tyranny.'[31] He added, 'I know no country in which there is in general less independence of mind and true freedom of discussion than in America. ... At first sight one might suppose that all American minds were formed on the same model, so likely are they to follow exactly the same paths. ... A king's only power is material, moreover: it affects actions but has no way of influencing wills. In the majority, however, is vested a force that is moral as well as material, which shapes wills as much as actions and inhibits not only deeds but also the desire to do them. ... The Inquisition was never able to prevent the circulation in Spain of books contrary to the religion of the majority. In the United States the majority has such sway that it can do better: it has banished even the thought of publishing such books.'[32]

Without independent means of forming their opinions, voters are encouraged to invest in candidates in a perfectly casual manner. It is not reason that guides men but passions, as Machiavelli already had noted. People's passions are here channelled towards the inessential. Candidates themselves constantly invoke emotional factors or 'spectacular' details of no significance. By personalising political life, the importance of platforms and ideas has been reduced to a minimum. In a television duel the candidate who wins is not the one who is promoting the best ideas, but the one who is the cleverest in presenting his opinions, who makes the best impression in terms of appearance, who comes across as the most quick-witted and 'telegenic', etc. Through a party, voters channel their votes towards someone they simply appreciate for his *image* and fame. A politician's image will clearly be tailored

---

30 *Gleichschaltung*, roughly meaning 'coordination', is a German term which refers to enforced social conformity and the removal of all opposition to the state. Initially a term used in electrical engineering, the term was infamously applied to politics by the National Socialists to describe their form of social organisation. (Ed.)

31 *Op. cit.*, p. 290. (Ed.)

32 *Op. cit.*, pp. 293-297. (Ed.)

to suit people's 'demand'. As for fame, this does not sanction particular qualities as much as reflect the more general 'stir' the person in question has managed to generate around himself. (It is preferable for a politician to have people speak ill of him than to ignore him: in the world of media, silence kills.) In these conditions, it is difficult to see what positive contribution the media may be making to the process of elections. Who was it who said that with the advent of democracy, *vanity* replaced zeal?

It has sometimes been suggested that widespread instantaneous access to information would make it possible in the modern age to adopt to certain forms of direct democracy. 'As the speed of information increases', Marshall McLuhan writes, 'the tendency is for politics to move away from representation and delegation of constituents toward immediate involvement of the entire community in the central acts of decision.'[33] Alvin Toffler holds the same opinion.[34] This idea, which is clearly connected to the *technical* ideology of the 'end of ideologies', is not very convincing. The crucial element in direct democracy is not the instantaneousness of information, but the *value* of information (which only in certain cases is linked to instantaneousness). Now, the new communication technologies do not improve the value of information; rather, they make its defects more immediately perceivable. The problem of the structuring and composition of information remains, as does the identity and intentions of the people delivering it. Not even pluralism can serve as a guarantee in this respect: for competition among media tends to lead to their standardisation. Ultimately, each medium is the message itself, *regardless of what its content may be*. (The real 'content' of a message is always the message itself.) Even assuming information 'transparency' is something desirable, it appears impossible to achieve.

The practice of *polling* is likewise hardly compatible with democracy. In theory, polls are meant to measure the statistical distribution of 'opinions' at a given moment; in practice, they juggle with stereotypes which tend to turn into unchangeable data, if for no other reason than that they are published. *Travesties* imitating a procedure on the basis of samples deemed to be 'representative', polls are falsely presented as

---

33 Marshall McLuhan, *Understanding Media* (New York: McGraw-Hill, 1964), p. 152. (Ed.)

34 Alvin Toffler, *The Third Wave* (New York: Morrow, 1980), pp. 427-430. (Ed.)

being analogous to reality or even more real than reality itself.[35] On the other hand, polling measures the intensity of individual preferences even less than elections do, as it merely translates the 'opinion' individuals would express *if they were to express their views*—without ever evaluating this possibility. Opinions collected through polls are thus treated as convictions, although they are not. 'Citizens must choose but cannot decide. It is this impotence which surveys both exploit and conceal. ... This method ignores all those conditions that determine people's stances, thus turning choices into timeless proposals.'[36]

'The distinguishing characteristic of our current public life is boredom', Pierre Viansson-Ponté wrote in the pages of *Le Monde* on 15 March 1968. 'The true aim of politics', he added, 'is not to govern the public good in the least bad way, but to lead to some form of progress or, at any rate, not to hinder it and to reflect the evolution which is bound to take place through laws and edicts. At a higher level, its aim is to guide the people, open up new horizons and foster enthusiasm.'[37] Fifteen years later we are still far from this goal. As it evolves, the political life of liberal democracies is now experiencing an unprecedented wave of indifference and apathy. The number of abstainers is steadily on the rise and at times even surpasses the number of voters. Richard Nixon was elected President of the United States with 26 per cent of the votes of registered voters (and only 43.4 per cent of the votes given); France approved the entrance of the United Kingdom into the Common Market in April 1972 with votes from only 36.11 per cent of its total voters, and so on. What should we make of a political majority that has not even been elected by the majority of those entitled to vote? The spread of apathy strips the very notions of legitimacy, representation and sovereignty of their meaning.

Ultimately, political apathy is not due to people being unaccustomed to voting, to poverty, illiteracy or lack of information; on the contrary, all these factors contribute to diminish it. Rather, it is due to the degeneration of politics in the Western world and to an increasingly

---

35 This will always be found to be the case when we compare polls and election results. Still, there are 'specialists' who will argue that polls could conveniently replace elections.

36 Pierre Rolle, 'Démocratie contre sondocratie', in *En Jeu*, September 1984.

37 This article, entitled 'France is Bored', has not been translated. (Ed.)

widespread feeling of impotence among voters *vis-à-vis* what is really at stake and the real nature of power.

In the absence of great events capable of exercising psychological pressure on voters and making 'extraordinary' characters stand out, in the context of a ruling ideology that is all the more powerful because it does not present itself as such, political evolution is leading to a 'narrowing down' of discourse and platforms, which are growing increasingly similar. This evolution today would appear to be accelerating. As a consequence, electoral power relations are increasingly reminiscent of random statistical data. In the case of a final ballot between two candidates, the result is invariably in the 50/50 range: it is increasingly unusual for elections to be won or lost by more than a tiny percentage of votes. All this leads to disastrous consequences. Elected candidates must govern with the greatest prudence so as not to lose even a fraction of their electorate (and this, of course, discourages them from taking any unpopular measures). At the same time, candidates will be tempted to win over a part of the electorate of other politicians (and this discourages them from implementing their own platforms). More and more voters, then, feel that politicians are all saying the same things and that Right-wing governments are adopting Left-wing policies (and vice-versa). The 'six of one and half-dozen of the other' formula is becoming increasingly common, and this only strengthens people's indifference and disgust. Majorities gained by a few hundred or even tens of thousands of votes are unstable and tenuous, and no longer express the general will. They reflect not so much a choice as a lack of choice, which is the very negation of the democratic ideal. 'May we still speak of democracy when the majority of citizens can no longer distinguish between the arguments of the opposition and those of the politicians in power?' (Claude Julien).

Other factors further contribute to this 'narrowing down'. The influence of economic and social concerns, linked to the spread of *economism*, leads to a depoliticisation of politics: the only debates taking place are those among 'managers' armed with statistics—and the effect is demotivation. Out of demagogy and a concern to please, candidates all end up saying much the same things to everyone, and their organisations turn into 'free-for-all' parties. Platforms are increasingly being based on surveys, which clearly give everyone the same results. It is thus getting harder and harder to distinguish the options presented by one party from those of the others. The impression is that parties are all striving for the same goal and the same model of society, differing only (to some extent) in terms of the means they are suggesting we adopt.

Given these conditions, people feel that freedom of choice is nothing but bait. Voters have realised that they are being offered a choice *within* a set of alternatives, but no actual *choice of alternatives*. *Agendas* determine referendums and the similarity between opposite poles limits one's range of choices. The situation is rather absurd: never has man been so free to choose as now that his range of choices has so narrowly been defined. Voters are free to opt among different parties because they are prevented from opting among different ideas—for these 'different' parties are increasingly *reasoning* all in the same way. Consequently, Western man has never been more rightfully indifferent towards the 'liberties' he enjoys—although his illusion of having these liberties shackles his will to rebel.

The talk going on about the 'complexity of problems' or the 'constraints' of the present situation further seems to suggest that politics is *no longer a matter of choice* and that the best voters can do is to let 'technicians' handle things, or more generally 'those in the know'. The opinion of 'experts' (something we previously discussed) carries far more weight than that of voters. Political apathy is thus becoming widespread.

The very notion of plurality becomes relative when it is applied to political parties. No doubt, there is in theory a distinction between single-party and multi-party systems, if for no other reason than that single parties are always state parties (whereas multiple parties reflect civil society).[38] Yet, it is equally true that practically all parties profess the same ideology and claim to pursue the same goal; hence one would be justified in arguing that the ruling system is that of a 'single-party' of which the political formations occupying the parliament merely represent competing tendencies. This impression is further reinforced

---

38 It has also been argued that there is little difference between a single-party system and a system with no parties, as by definition the former does away with the notion of opposition that is characteristic of party systems. On the other hand, someone like Spengler reckons that single-party systems have all the inconveniences of multi-party ones. Let us not forget, however, that in the Third World, the establishment of democracy has often coincided with that of a single-party, considered (not without reason at times) to be the most adequate way of bringing people together in the pursuit of a common goal (see Édouard Kodjo, 'Pour le parti unique', in *Jeune Afrique*, 20 January 1970).

in those cases where fewer differences exist between the members of two parties than between two given members of the same party (as is often the case with the Republican and Democratic parties in the U.S.). One might also envisage a single-party system in which the overall differences among the various currents of the party are greater than those found among different parties in multi-party systems. After all, the rivalries among leaders of single-party systems can be just as fierce as those opposing the leaders of different parties in classic parliamentary regimes.

A final factor that contributes to political apathy is politicians' lack of imagination (or ambition) and of any grand plans. 'In every age', Tocqueville writes, 'it is important for those who rule nations to act with an eye to the future, but this is even more important in democratic and unbelieving centuries.'[39] Unfortunately, it is also harder in these ages. The short duration of electoral mandates encourages politicians to focus on short-term goals. The rise of *economism* takes place at the expense of 'grand politics'. In a society pervaded by the ideal of egalitarianism, the very notions of grandeur and collective destiny raise suspicion. Finally, grand plans are in a way antithetical to the legal fetishism of the liberal state. Static by definition, juridical institutions are hardly suited to the pursuit of truly historic actions.[40]

Political apathy, then, fosters *negative* voting. As political platforms no longer stir any enthusiasm, and as no politician appears capable of obtaining any 'good results', voters content themselves with stopping those candidates they are less fond of or even systematically punishing the 'outgoing' candidate. Instead of voting for politicians, they vote *against* them.[41] In a democratic system that is already itself treated as the 'least bad' system rather than the *best*, voting is only used to prevent the 'worst'. Hence, voting is not indicative of any clear orientation.

---

39 *Op. cit.*, p. 640. (Ed.)

40 In this respect, one might draw a contrast between 'nomocracies' (in which law is supreme) and 'telocracies' (in which goals are supreme). The latter strictly depend on political will and, more generally, on the 'constructivism' Hayek publicly reviled (see Bertrand de Jouvenel, 'Sur l'étude des formes de gouvernement', in *Bulletin SEDEIS*, 20 April 1961).

41 As is well-known, it would be more accurate to say that in France in 1981 Giscard was defeated than Mitterrand elected. It is just as revealing that the widespread disfavour the policies of the socialist government are now enjoying is not benefitting opposition parties.

At most, it allows people to slow down a given trend—which is not exactly the most efficient way of making progress.

Liberal authors, who are distrustful of popular sovereignty and prefer to rely on 'experts', have often argued that political apathy is something good. They interpret it as a factor of 'stability' connected to the rise of the middle class, which is held to be intrinsically less 'politicised' than the others. Widespread political engagement is thus regarded as a potential threat, as it borders on 'activism'. Francesco Nitti went so far as to write that 'only the existence of a large middle class is a safeguard for democratic stability'[42]—despite the fact that in his day the middle classes accounted for most of the support enjoyed by Fascism! More recently, in the United States, Seymour Martin Lipset[43] and W. H. Morris-Jones[44] have argued that political apathy represents an excellent bulwark against pressure from extremists.[45]

This is a most specious way of reasoning. Far from being 'an effective counter-force to the fanatics',[46] apathy plays in their favour: for under these conditions, 'fanatics' may easily be the only ones capable of mobilising public opinion. The prevalence of greyness brings out colours—whatever they may be. When political life is in decline, violence and terrorism appear as the only means of striking an anaesthetised public opinion with no power over legal procedures. Apathy is a real gift to extremism. Similarly, if all controversies surrounding genuine problems and stakes cannot be addressed in the framework of classic institutions and regular proceedings, they are bound to erupt anarchically elsewhere. As 'politicians' politics' has turned into a simple matter of management, politics tends to resurface in other circles, which are rarely subject to voting. If no legitimate channels can be

---

42 *Op. cit.*, vol. 1, p. 52.

43 *Political Man: The Social Bases of Politics* (Garden City, New York: Doubleday, 1960).

44 'In Defence of Apathy: Some Doubts on the Duty to Vote', in *Political Studies*, vol. 2, no. 1, February 1954. Available online at onlinelibrary.wiley.com/doi/10.1111/j.1467-9248.1954.tb01011.x/pdf (accessed 15 November 2010). W. H. Morris-Jones was actually British, not American. (Ed.)

45 Moses I. Finley's book *Democracy Ancient and Modern* (*op. cit.*) is largely devoted to a refutation of the arguments advanced by Lipset and Morris-Jones. Finley often takes a polemical and biased approach, but his criticism of political apathy hits the target.

46 Morris-Jones, *op. cit.*, p. 37. (Ed.)

found to express given aspirations, a different path will be sought. The talk made of 'auxiliary democracy' is revealing in this respect.

In practice, the main effect of political apathy is that it gives a free hand to those really in power (which is the reason why certain dictatorships also encourage 'depoliticisation'). Liberals who commend it seek to legitimise the idea of a technocratic society in which decisions no longer obey democratic criteria of legitimacy. In doing so, they are eliciting reactions of rejection the consequences of which are impossible to foresee. The degeneration of democracy may lead to democracy's end. 'What I would chiefly criticise the present political class for', Michel Debré declares, 'is the fact that it fills men attached to democracy with doubts.'[47]

Jean-Paul Sartre[48] has gone so far as to claim that universal suffrage is of no democratic value: 'All kinds of electoral systems constitute the set of electors as a passive material for other-direction; and the election results no more represent the will of the country, than the top ten records represent the taste of the customers.'[49] In May 1968[50] this position was summed up by the slogan 'Elections, a trap for idiots'.

Scepticism has only grown since then. According to Claude Julien, 'Universal suffrage and the—largely theoretical—separation of powers are not enough to ensure the democratic character of society. The latter is affected by many other forces that no one would dare describe as democratically organised. ... If democratic life has grown feeble, this is mostly because its fundamental institution—elections—does not allow citizens to make clear choices and exercise their responsibility as the depositories of national sovereignty .... As it is being applied, universal suffrage does not enable citizens to choose their own destinies

---

47 In *Magazine-Hebdo*, 19 October 1984.

48 Jean-Paul Sartre (1905-1980) was a philosopher who, with the possible exception of Martin Heidegger (who resisted the label), was the chief formulator of the philosophy which came to be known as existentialism. He was also a Marxist. (Ed.)

49 Jean-Paul Sartre, *Critique of Dialectical Reason*, vol. 1 (New York: Verso, 2004), p. 654.

50 May 1968 was when a series of strikes by radical Left-wing student groups in Paris were joined by the majority of the French workforce, shutting down France and nearly bringing down the government of Charles de Gaulle. Although the strikes ended in failure and had evaporated by July, they are still seen as the decisive moment when traditional French society was forced to give way to the more liberal attitude that has come to define France in subsequent years. (Ed.)

and does not oblige parties to pursue clear platforms. It allows candidates to sidestep burning issues, and even encourages them to hide behind general arguments. It does not treat them as the genuine representatives of clearly expressed national sovereignty; in fact, it does not even lend them any rigorous democratic sanction *post facto*. ... Democracy is ill because citizens are not giving their vote to politicians from whom they expect a concrete course of action reflecting well-defined commitments. Voting is no longer a positive act by which citizens make their own will known and bestow a mandate for rule on elected politicians so that they may implement this will. Rather, it is essentially a negative act by which citizens instead of adhering to a constructive platform choose the lesser evil.'[51]

Serge-Christophe Kolm sums up his view of elections as follows: 'It is a systematic hold up of the rights of the people. It is large-scale pillaging of popular sovereignty, which demolishes the very foundations of the principle of legitimacy behind the official ideology of our society .... Ultimately, elections are a masquerade through which the bourgeoisie gains the consensus of the people, a great legitimacy-bestowing class ceremony through which the sceptre of power is laid at the feet of one of the heralds of the bourgeoisie, a national psychodrama of general abdication that distracts, puts to sleep and mystifies the subject and contented masses. What a wonderful exchange: a ballot in the ballot-box once every few years and the masters' voices from the television box the rest of the time. The people does not choose its politicians, it anoints them.'[52]

Lamartine[53] used to say that 'universal suffrage is democracy'. In the light of what we have noted so far, his is a rather questionable claim. On the one hand, as we have seen, all forms of power must take into account the opinion of the majority if they are to endure. On the other, from a historical and theoretical point of view, the notion of

---

51 *Op. cit.*, pp. 112-137.

52 *Op. cit.*, pp. 134-135.

53 Alphonse de Lamartine (1790-1869) was a liberal and pacifist writer and politician, regarded as the first French Romantic poet. He announced the formation of the Second Republic in 1848. The exact passage De Benoist is referring to reads, '...universal suffrage was the right of the sovereignty of the people, or of the sovereignty of opinion, or of the sovereignty of the national reason. It is the same thing', in *The Past, Present, and Future of the Republic* (New York: Harper & Brothers, 1850), p. 125. (Ed.)

democracy does not appear to be indissolubly linked to elections. Plato lists seven factors that in his opinion bestow the right to govern, but never mentions elections.[54] Aristotle believes that voting is nothing but a ploy. Only with Montesquieu was it argued for the first time that 'voting by lot is in the nature of democracy'.[55] In the Twentieth century, political theorist Carl Schmitt[56] argued that democracy should be distinguished from parliamentarianism, as the latter is rooted not in the democratic tradition but in the liberal one.[57]

A contemporary socialist, Julien Cheverny, writes, 'Elections represent neither democracy as a whole nor its central feature. Far from being a necessary and sufficient condition for democracy, elections contribute to destroy and degrade it .... By subjecting its electoral system to the law of sheer numbers, abstract democracy is ignoring the factor of continuity among different generations, social categories, values and interests which represents the driving force behind all political regimes, if not their very constitutive element. By becoming identified with elections—practically the only method used nowadays to appoint governments and the people in charge—democracy is not only eschewing other selection procedures more suited to its spirit; it is also unintentionally favouring the reign of hazard and force more than the progress of reason and law.'[58]

---

54 *Laws*, Book Three.

55 *Op. cit.*, p. 13. (Ed.)

56 Carl Schmitt (1888-1985) was an important German jurist who wrote about political science, geopolitics and constitutional law. He was part of the Conservative Revolutionary metapolitical movement of the Weimar era. He also briefly supported the National Socialists at the beginning of their regime, although they later turned against him. He remains highly influential in the fields of law and philosophy. (Ed.)

57 See his 1922 book *Political Theology* (Chicago: University of Chicago Press, 2005) and his 1926 book *The Crisis of Parliamentary Democracy* (Cambridge: MIT Press, 1985).

58 *Haro sur la démocratie*, p. 77.

V

TOWARDS ORGANIC DEMOCRACY

There is one point on which Montesquieu and Rousseau agree—namely, that a state's form of government should be suited to its territorial extension and the size of its population.[1] 'If the natural property of small states is to be governed as republics', Montesquieu writes, 'that of medium-sized ones, to be subject to a monarch, and that of large empires to be dominated by a despot'.[2] Rousseau, like most minds behind the French Revolution, held it to be axiomatic that a republic or democracy could not be established on a vast territory inhabited by a large number of citizens. The more numerous the members of a society, Rousseau argued, the stronger should its government be.[3] This statement agrees with what the history of ancient democracy would appear to suggest. The population of Athens only occupied a territory the size of Luxembourg, and the number of its male citizens never rose above 40,000 or 45,000.

---

1   'A more frequent use of referendums might serve as a genuinely democratic way of balancing the representative system', Bernard Chenot, the honorary Vice President of the French Council of State, noted on 10 December 1984 at a meeting of the Academy of Moral and Political Sciences. 'Certainly', he added, 'history shows the risks of popular elections … This would no longer be a valid objection if referendum initiatives were more equally divided and if the questions posed concerned not a given person or policy but rather a text, in such a way as to fix legislative principles through a sort of outline law.'

2   *Op. cit.*, p. 126. (Ed.)

3   *The Social Contract*, Book Three, Chapter One, texts 13 and 15.

Aristotle, too, asserts that democracy cannot exist in a 'state composed of too many people'.[4]

Modern experience has led to a different point of view. Yet it is still the prevalent opinion that *direct* democracy can only be implemented in small political units. Indeed, one may argue with Giovanni Sartori that the degree to which self-government is feasible is inversely proportional to the extension of its field of application and the span of time taken into consideration.

On the other hand, it may be observed that the nature of 'government'—or 'power', as we would say nowadays—has undergone significant changes. Power is more diffused: decisions are now taken simultaneously by different authorities. 'Great societies' are comprised of a multitude of associations and communities. If we wish to rediscover the spirit of direct democracy, it is primarily at this level that we must seek to organise political participation. Municipal associations, intermediate bodies, regional assemblies and professional bodies are all areas in which it is perfectly possible today to foster popular initiatives, collective 'interest' and local, 'grassroots', democracy.

The promotion of referendums represents another way of exercising direct democracy which is perfectly compatible with the requirements of modern living. Still, plebiscites, which both Napoleon III[5] and General de Gaulle[6] used considerably, have received much criticism. The very word 'plebiscite' has acquired negative connotations. One objection that is frequently raised is that the conditions in which plebiscites take place are often far from ideal. But this argument should not lead us to reject plebiscites as such. These referendums are highly democratic procedures that allow governments to ascertain at any time whether their decisions agree (or not) with the general will. This is the very principle Sieyès[7] formulated: 'Authority comes from above, confidence from below'.

---

4   *Politics*, Book Seven, Chapter Four, 1326b3.

5   In the early years of Napoleon III's reign, his regime frequently manipulated elections and otherwise stifled democracy, until he liberalised in an effort to bolster his waning popularity. (Ed.)

6   In 1962, de Gaulle altered the French Constitution to allow elections to take place by direct universal suffrage for the first time since 1848, which allowed him to avert defeat. (Ed.)

7   Emmanuel-Joseph Sieyès (1748-1836) was a clergyman who became one of the chief theorists of the French Revolution in 1789. His pamphlet, *What Is the Third*

Answering those who like to recall how certain dictators favoured the use of plebiscites, Georges Burdeau writes, 'While it is frequently the case that dictatorships are established by popular acclamation, they only endure through the silence of the people.' He adds, 'With plebiscitary democracy ... not only are men free, but the government itself is based on this freedom, since it is from suffrage that the leader derives his power. Certainly, a free hand is given through voting ... but the fact remains that voters have chosen a leader for themselves and confirmed their support of him, and it is on this which the latter's authority is legally founded. On what basis, by invoking the ideal of democracy, can one condemn this use of suffrage as opposed to all others? None, really.'[8]

Certain flaws attributed to referendums could be corrected by redefining their modes of application. The date and content of certain questions, for instance, might be settled beforehand. A distinction must also be drawn between referendums launched by heads of state and popular referendums, for which approval from a fixed quota of citizens must first be reached (as in the Swiss model). The promotion of referendums of the latter sort in France, as well as elsewhere, would restore a sense of reciprocity in the relations between the governing authorities and citizens, reinforcing the direct links between the two which are already strengthened by the direct appointment of the head of state through universal suffrage. Referendums would thus serve as a perfect modern embodiment of the 'popular acclamation' that was once used to express consensus.

Following Carl Schmitt's suggestions, an attempt might also be made to create qualitative—as opposed to merely quantitative—procedures for measuring consensus. Here, too, the aim would be to establish a direct link between the government and those governed whenever possible, in such a way as to reinforce the mutual *identification* between the people and decision-makers, in line with the idea of *embodied democracy*.

Ultimately, it is a matter of exploring all possibilities of creating *new ways for citizens to participate in public life*. After all, the key notion for democracy is not numbers, suffrage, elections or representation, but *participation*. This notion is to be assumed in all of its

---

Estate?, became an important manifesto of the Revolution. (Ed.)

8   *La démocratie,* pp. 59-60.

various meanings. Participation means to take part: in other words, to put oneself to the test as the member of a community, as *part of a whole*, and to take up the *active* role this identity implies. An excellent definition is provided by René Capitant: 'Participation is the individual act of a citizen acting as a member of a community of people'.[9] Participation lends *sanction* to one's identity as a member of a community, while at the same time *resulting* from this identity; again, it is this identity which it actively *crystallises* in specific acts. Participation is a *right*, but it is also a service and, in a way, a *duty*. In his funeral oration, Pericles states, 'Unlike other nations, we regard him who takes no part in politics not as unambitious or peaceful, but as a useless citizen.'[10]

Democracy, in its most essential features thus stands in open contrast to the liberal legitimisation of political apathy, which it is difficult not to regard as a negation of popular sovereignty. But democracy is also incompatible with liberal principles in other respects. As a form of political authority, democracy cannot accept that this be made subject to the control of the economy and of its representatives. Democracy is founded on the principle of equality of political rights, which is something quite different from the belief in the natural equality of beings. Finally, it bases political rights on citizenship, therefore implying that individuals are primarily defined by their identity as belonging to a community. There can be no democracy without a people, a nation, or city—since these are not transient structures or insignificant conglomerates, but the choice settings for democratic practice. Democracy is simply that form of government in which the greatest number of people can take part in public life. So it is not institutions that make democracy, but rather the people's participation in institutions. Popular sovereignty is expressed through everyone's participation. The maximum of democracy coincides with the maximum of popular participation.

In words that have become famous, Moeller van den Bruck defined democracy as 'a folk's participation in its own destiny'.[11] He added, 'What makes a state democratic is not its form of government, but people's participation in this government.' This conception implies elite turnover. A true democracy is not so much a regime in which

---

9   *Op. cit.*, p. 36.

10   From Thucydides, *History of the Peloponnesian War,* Book Two, text 40. (Ed.)

11   'Democratie ist Anteilnahme eines Volkes an seinem Schicksal' (*Gewissen,* 3 June 1922).

everyone can vote as a system in which everyone, proportionately to his merit, has the same chances of accessing power. 'We have a genuine democracy when the circle from which leaders are recruited is as large as possible, not when the greatest possible number of people can contribute to decision-making with their votes.'[12]

Universal suffrage has few of the defects it is accused of having. But certainly it does not exhaust all the possibilities of democracy; indeed, it may not even be its chief embodiment. Citizenship is not simply expressed through voting, and the rule of the majority is not the only procedure to measure the consensus enjoyed by governments or people's support of their leaders' actions. Political participation, in other words, cannot be reduced to voting power. The people should be given the chance to decide wherever they can; and wherever they cannot, it should be given the chance to lend or deny its consent. Decentralisation, the delegating of responsibilities, retroactive consent and plebiscites are all procedures that may be combined with universal suffrage. There is no reason to believe that any one of these procedures is better than the rest. Elections, too, may be combined with other local or national procedures, as 'voting works best in groups that have operated a preliminary selection of their members' (Jules Cheverny).

Against liberal democracy and tyrannical forms of 'popular democracy', we should return to a conception of popular sovereignty based on the historical sources of genuine democracy. All too often nowadays do we draw a contrast between 'liberty' and 'equality'. Rather, we should attempt to redefine both these terms.

Liberal democracy quite rightly considers liberty as the foundation of democracy, but the way it defines it is most questionable. 'Popular democracy', on the other hand, rightly stresses the idea of popular sovereignty, which it nonetheless defines in terms just as misleading. The common denominator between these two forms of modern democracy is egalitarian individualism, from which both the 'liberty' of liberals and 'the people' of supporters of popular democracy stem. Democracy must instead rediscover the meaning which the inventors of Greek democracy assigned to the notions of *people* and *liberty*.

---

12 Edgar Julius Jung, 'Volkserhaltung', in *Deutsche Rundschau*, 1930, p. 188. Jung (1894-1934) was a lawyer who was also one of the principal writers of the Conservative Revolutionary movement in Weimar Germany. He was killed by the Nazis during the Night of the Long Knives. His main work is *The Rule of the Inferiour* (Lewiston: Edwin Mellen Press, 1995), in two volumes. (Ed.)

Democracy must be founded not on the alleged inalienable rights of rootless individuals, but on citizenship, which sanctions one's belonging to a given folk—that is, a culture, history and destiny—and to the political structure within which it has developed. Liberty results from one's identity as a member of a folk: the liberty of the folk commands all other liberties. In genuine democracies, citizens only possess equal political rights as members of the same national and folk community. The abstract egalitarian principle 'one man, one vote' must be replaced with the more realistic and concrete principle 'one citizen, one vote'.

A democracy based not on the idea of rootless individuals or 'humanity' but on the *folk* as a collective organism and privileged historical agent might be termed an *organic democracy*. It would represent the logical evolution of Greek democracy, and of a current of thought that places at the centre of social and political life notions such as those of mutual aid, the harmony of opposites, analogy, the geometry of proportions, the dialectic between authority and consent, the equality of political rights, participation, and the mutual identification of governments with those governed.[13]

The idea of *fraternity* might provide a basis for this redefinition of popular sovereignty. It is certainly the case that this was only a vague term in the past. It has chiefly been used to mean assistance, charitable aid, 'humanism', philanthropy and 'universal peace', or even 'love' and 'charity'—all notions with a strong Christian ring to them. Rather than its *national* dimension, it is the hypothetically transnational dimension of fraternity that has most often been stressed: 'All men are brothers', Pierre Leroux[14] writes; and this is what makes Moses the 'lawgiver of fraternity'. Yet, Michelet[15] had intended to write a history

---

13 Joseph Görres, Schleiermacher and Schelling, to mention but a few names, are all representatives of this current of thought. In Spain, organic democracy—as opposed to individualist and representative democracy—has been theorised in modern times by exponents of the 'Krausist' socialist Left such as Julian Besteiro and Fernando de Los Rios (see Gonzalo Fernàndez de la Mora, 'Teoricos socialistas de la democracia organica', in *Razón española*, August 1984, pp. 203-213).

14 Pierre Leroux (1797-1871) was a philosopher who advocated democracy, pantheistic spirituality, and humanitarianism. He is also credited with introducing the term 'socialism' to France. His work is untranslated. (Ed.)

15 Jules Michelet (1798-1874) was a historian and man of letters. The book De Benoist refers to is the two-volume *History of France* (New York: D. Appleton, 1845-1851). (Ed.)

of France as a 'history of fraternity'—and not without reason. For to the idea that 'fraternity knows no fatherland' one may object that, on the contrary, it does. Fatherlands are the natural settings of fraternity whenever this is used to express one's duty towards those who share his heritage. Humanity is necessarily pluralistic. It presents incompatible value systems. It is comprised of different families—and does not constitute a family in itself ('species' is a biological notion with no historical or cultural value). The only 'families' in which genuinely 'fraternal' relations may be entertained are cultures, peoples and nations. Fraternity, therefore, can serve as the basis for both solidarity and social justice, for both patriotism and democratic participation.

The founding motto of the French Republic consists of three words: Liberty, Equality, and Fraternity.[16] Curiously, though, the notion of fraternity was not included in the Declaration of 1789, in the Constitutions of 1791 and 1793, or in the Charter of 1830. Liberal democracies have exploited the word *liberty*. 'Popular democracies' have seized the word *equality*. Organic democracy, founded on national and popular sovereignty, might be the democracy of *fraternity*.

---

16 On the various historical and semantic embodiments of these three terms, see Gérald Antoine, '*Liberté-Égalité-Fraternité*', *ou, Les fluctuations d'une devise* (Paris: UNESCO, 1981).

POSTFACE:
TEN THESES ON DEMOCRACY

1. Since everyone nowadays claims to be a democrat, democracy is defined in several mutually contradictory ways. The etymological approach is misleading. To define democracy on the basis of the modern regimes which have (rather belatedly) proclaimed themselves to be democratic is questionable to say the least. The historical approach ultimately appears to be the most reasonable: to attempt to define democracy, one must first know what it meant for those who invented it. Ancient democracy brings together a community of citizens in an assembly, granting them equal political rights. The notions of citizenship, liberty, popular sovereignty and equal rights are all closely interconnected. Liberty stems from one's identity as a member of a people, which is to say from one's origins. This is liberty as participation. The liberty of the folk commands all other liberties; common interest prevails over particular interests. Equality of rights derives from the status as an equal citizen enjoyed by all free men. It is a political tool. The essential difference between ancient democracies and modern ones is the fact that the former do not know the egalitarian individualism on which the latter are founded.

2. Liberalism and democracy are not synonyms. Democracy is a '-cracy', which is to say a form of political power, whereas liberalism is an ideology for the limitation of all political power. Democracy is based on popular sovereignty; liberalism, on the rights

of the individual. Liberal representative democracy implies the delegation of sovereignty, which strictly speaking—as Rousseau had realised—is tantamount to abdication by the people. In a representative system, the people elect representatives who govern by themselves: the electorate legitimises a genuine power which lies exclusively in the hands of representatives. In a genuine system of popular sovereignty, elected candidates are only entrusted with expressing the will of the people and the nation; they do not embody it.

3. Many arguments can be raised against the classic critique of democracy as the reign of incompetence and the 'dictatorship of numbers'. Democracy should neither be confused with the reign of numbers nor with the majority principle. Its underlying principle is rather a 'holistic' one, namely: acknowledgement of the fact that the people, as such, hold political prerogatives. The equality of rights does not reflect any natural equality; rather, it is a right deriving from citizenship, the exercise of which is what enables individual participation. Numerical equality must be distinguished from the geometrical view, which respects proportions. The purpose of majority rule is not to determine the truth; it is merely to choose among different options. Democracy does not stand in contrast to the idea of strong power any more than it stands in contrast to the notions of authority, selection or elite.

4. There is a difference between the notion of generic competence and specific competence. If the people have all the necessary information, it is perfectly capable of judging whether it is being well-governed or not. The emphasis placed on 'competence' nowadays—where this word is increasingly understood to mean 'technical knowledge'—is extremely ambiguous. Political competence has to do not with knowledge but with decision-making, as Max Weber has shown in his works on scientists and politicians. The idea that the best government is that of 'scientists' or 'experts' betrays a complete lack of understanding of politics; when applied, it generally leads to catastrophic results. Today this idea is being used to legitimise technocracy, whereby power—in accordance

with the technical ideology and belief in the 'end of ideologies' —becomes intrinsically opposed to popular sovereignty.

5. In a democratic system, citizens all hold equal political rights not by virtue of any alleged inalienable rights possessed by the 'human person', but because they all belong to the same national and folk community—which is to say, by virtue of their citizenship. At the basis of democracy lies not the idea of 'society', but of a community of citizens who are all heirs to the same history and/or wish to carry this history on towards a common destiny. The fundamental principle behind democracy is not 'one man, one vote', but 'one citizen, one vote'.

6. The key notion for democracy is not numbers, suffrage, elections or representation, but participation. 'Democracy is a folk's participation in its own destiny' (Moeller van den Bruck). It is that form of government which acknowledges each citizen's right to take part in public affairs, particularly by appointing the government and lending or denying his consent to it. So it is not institutions that make democracy, but rather the people's participation in institutions. The maximum of democracy coincides not with the 'maximum of liberty' or the 'maximum of equality', but with the maximum of participation.

7. The majority principle is adopted because unanimity, which the notions of general will and popular sovereignty imply in theory, is in practice impossible to achieve. The notion of majority can be treated as either a dogma (in which case it is a substitute for unanimity) or as a technique (in which case it is an expedient). Only the latter view assigns a relative value to the minority or opposition, as this may become tomorrow's majority. Its adoption raises the question of the field of application of pluralism and of its limits. We should not confuse the pluralism of opinions, which is legitimate, with the pluralism of values, which proves to be incompatible with the very notion of the people. Pluralism finds its limit in subordination to the common good.

8. The evolution of modern liberal democracies, which are elective polyarchies, clearly reflects the degeneration of the democratic

ideal. Parties do not operate democratically as institutions. The tyranny of money rigs competition and engenders corruption. Mass voting prevents individual votes from proving decisive. Elected candidates are not encouraged to keep their commitments. Majority vote does not take account of the intensity of people's preferences. Opinions are not formed independently: information is both biased (which prevents the free determination of choices) and standardised (which reinforces the tyranny of public opinion). The trend towards the standardising of political platforms and arguments makes it increasingly difficult to distinguish between different options. Political life thus becomes purely negative and universal suffrage comes to be perceived as an illusion. The result is political apathy, a principle that is the opposite of participation, and hence democracy.

9. Universal suffrage does not exhaust the possibilities of democracy: there is more to citizenship than voting. A return to political procedures in keeping with the original spirit of democracy requires an assessment of all those practices which reinforce the direct link between people and their government and extend local democracy, for instance: the fostering of participation through municipal and professional assemblies, the spread of popular initiatives and referendums, and the development of qualitative methods for expressing consent. In contrast to liberal democracies and tyrannical 'popular democracies', which invoke the notions of liberty, equality and the people, organic democracy might be centred on the idea of fraternity.

10. Democracy means the power of the people, which is to say the power of an organic community that has historically developed in the context of one or more given political structures—for instance a city, nation, or empire. Where there is no folk but only a collection of individual social atoms, there can be no democracy. Every political system which requires the disintegration or levelling of peoples in order to operate—or the erosion of individuals' awareness of belonging to an organic folk community—is to be regarded as undemocratic.

Other books published by Arktos:

Fighting for the Essence
by Pierre Krebs

Beyond Human Rights
by Alain de Benoist

Revolution from Above
by Kerry Bolton

The Owls of Afrasiab
by Lars Holger Holm

The WASP Question
by Andrew Fraser

Why We Fight
by Guillaume Faye

De Naturae Natura
by Alexander Jacob

It Cannot Be Stormed
by Ernst von Salomon

The Saga of the Aryan Race
by Porus Homi Havewala

Against Democracy and Equality: The European New Right
by Tomislav Sunic

The Jedi in the Lotus
by Steven J. Rosen

Archeofuturism
by Guillaume Faye

A Handbook of Traditional Living

Tradition & Revolution
by Troy Southgate

Can Life Prevail?
A Revolutionary Approach to the Environmental Crisis
by Pentti Linkola

Metaphysics of War:
Battle, Victory & Death in the World of Tradition
by Julius Evola

The Path of Cinnabar: An Intellectual Autobiography
by Julius Evola

Journals published by Arktos:

The Initiate: Journal of Traditional Studies

CPSIA information can be obtained
at www.ICGtesting.com
Printed in the USA
BVHW030851241118
533886BV00001B/370/P